Walk Away

Walk Away

The Rise and Fall of the Home-Ownership Myth

Douglas E. French

Ludwig
von Mises
Institute

AUBURN, ALABAMA

Ludwig von Mises Institute
518 West Magnolia Avenue
Auburn, Alabama   36832

Ph: (334) 844-2500
Fax: (334) 844-2583

mises.org

10 9 8 7 6 5 4 3 2

ISBN: 978-1-61016-102-2

Contents

Introduction

The idea that "a man's house is his castle" is attributed to American Revolutionary James Otis from 1761, and his idea was that government should never be permitted to breach its walls. It is a good thought, in context; one that sums up a dogged attachment to the right of private property.

In the 20th century, however, government got behind the idea that every citizen should be provided a castle of his or her own. This is the essence of the good life, we were told, that very core of our material aspirations. The home is the most valuable possession we could ever have. It is the best investment, even better than gold. Government would make us all owners, one way or another, even if it meant violating rights to make it happen.

This became an article of faith, a central tenet of the American civic religion, and one that led to additional spin-off doctrines. We should fill our valuable homes with vast amounts of furniture, large pieces especially, things that suggest permanence and roots. If there were any doubt as to where to put our money, an answer was always ready: put it into our home, where it will surely pay the highest return.

The home itself could provide full-time employment for half of the American citizenry, as all women became "home makers" who devote themselves to cooking, laundry, and cleaning, while all extra time that the man had should be devoted to lawn care, household repairs, and landscaping. The home was the very foundation of community, of freedom, of the American dream. It embodied who we are and what we do.

Beginning in 2007 and culminating in 2008 this dream was smashed as home values all over the country plummeted, wiping out a primary means of savings. Some homes fell by as much as 75–80%, instilling shock and awe all across the country. The thing that was never supposed to happen had happened. This meant more than mere asset depreciation. An article of faith had fallen, and there were many spillover effects.

The home was the foundation of our financial strategy, our love of accumulating large things, the core of our strategic outlook for our lives. Once that goes, much more goes besides. The things in the home suddenly become devalued. We look around us in astonishment at how much stuff we have, and we are weighed down by the very prospect of moving. We are longing for a different way, perhaps for the first time in a century.

We are beginning to see the response in the new behavior of some younger people. The *New York Times*, the *Wall Street Journal*, and other major media outlets are starting to cover the trend of what we might call the new mobility. Young couples are selling off their possessions: their large furniture, their china and crystal, their enormous bedrooms suites, and even their cars. They are lightening the load, preparing for a life of mobility, even international mobility.

The collapse of the housing market—which has occurred despite every effort by the government to prevent it—coincides with the highest rate of unemployment among young people that we've seen in many generations. Economic opportunity is dwindling, at least in traditional jobs. The advance of digital technology has made it possible to do untraditional jobs while living anywhere, and perhaps changing one's location every year or two.

Millions have walked away from their mortgages. Those who have swear that they will never again be tricked by the great housing myth that this one asset is guaranteed to go up and up forever. The new source of value is not something attached to the biggest thing we own but rather in the most fundamental unit of all: ourselves, and what we can do. This change represents a dramatic change not just for one generation but for an entire ethos that has defined what it means to be an American for about a century.

To walk away might at first seem like a post-modern activity, one that disconnects us with history and community. We might just as easily see it as a recapturing and redefining of an older tradition that shaped the American ethos from the colonial period through the latter part of the 19th century: the pioneer spirit. Our ancestors moved freely, across great distances, beginning with oceans and then continuing across great masses of land, from New England to the West, all in search of economic opportunity and the fulfillment of a different American dream, defined by freedom itself.

This change begins with a single realization: I'm paying more for my house than my house is worth. What precisely is the downside of walking away, of going into a "strategic default"? I lose my house. Good. That's better than losing money on my house. But what are the economic and ethical implications of this? Americans haven't faced this dilemma in at least a century. But now they are, by the millions. They are awakening to the reality that the house is no different from any other physical possession. It has no magical properties and it embodies no high ideals. It is just sticks and bricks.

This book examines the background to the case of strategic default and considers its implications from a variety of different perspectives. The thesis here is that there is nothing ominous or evil about this practice. It is an extension of economic rationality.

But what about the idea that our home is our castle? My thesis is that the essence of freedom is to come to understand that the real castle is to be found within.

What is Strategic Default?

Strategic default is when homeowners stop paying on their mortgages when, in fact, they can afford to make payments, but choose not to because the house that serves as collateral for the loan is worth considerably less than the loan balance.

These are not people who take out a mortgage and never make a payment. Strategic defaulters borrowed the money in good faith to buy or refinance a home during the housing bubble of the mid-2000's. They made their payments until they realized it didn't make sense to feed a mortgage on a house worth a fraction of what they owe.

CBS's *60 Minutes* aired a story on strategic defaults in May of 2009 and estimated that a million homeowners who could pay chose to walk away instead. Nearly a third of all foreclosures in 2010 are believed to strategic defaults, up from 22 percent in the first quarter of 2009.

Academics like Professor Luigi Zingales at the University of Chicago worry that as more people strategic default, the stigma once attached to it will fall away, and "[t]he risk that the number of people doing this might explode is significant," says the professor.

A hypothetical example, created by Brent T. White in his Arizona *Legal Studies Discussion Paper*, would be that a young couple buys a 3-bedroom, 1380 square foot home in Salinas, California for $585,000 in January 2006, which was the average home price in Salinas at that

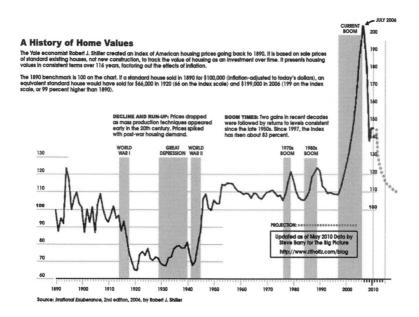

A History of Home Values

The Yale economist Robert J. Shiller created an index of American housing prices going back to 1890. It is based on sale prices of standard existing houses, not new construction, to track the value of housing as an investment over time. It presents housing values in consistent terms over 116 years, factoring out the effects of inflation.

The 1890 benchmark is 100 on the chart. If a standard house sold in 1890 for $100,000 (inflation-adjusted to today's dollars), an equivalent standard house would have sold for $66,000 in 1920 (66 on the index scale) and $199,000 in 2006 (199 on the index scale, or 99 percent higher than 1890).

DECLINE AND RUN-UP: Prices dropped as mass production techniques appeared early in the 20th century. Prices spiked with post-war housing demand.

BOOM TIMES: Two gains in recent decades were followed by returns to levels consistent since the late 1950s. Since 1997, the index has risen about 83 percent.

PROJECTION: Updated as of May 2010 Data by Steve Barry for The Big Picture
http://www.ritholtz.com/blog

Source: *Irrational Exuberance*, 2nd edition, 2006, by Robert J. Shiller

time. The couple had excellent credit and qualified for a no-money down fixed interest rate 30-year loan at 6.5% with a total payment of $4,300 per month (P & I, taxes, mortgage, and homeowners insurance). This was 31% of their gross monthly income and thus was considered affordable by the lender. With the couple's other living expenses they struggled to break even each month, but were comfortable stretching to make the purchase, believing the home would increase in value. And the lender was comfortable enough to make the loan.

Unfortunately the housing market collapsed and despite still owing $560,000 on their mortgage, the home securing that loan is only worth $187,000 four years later. There is a similar house in the same subdivision listed for $179,000. If they walk away and buy the similar house, with a 5% down payment of about $9,000—a couple of payments on the current underwater place—the total monthly payment would be $1,200 (compared to the $4,300 they pay now); or the couple could rent a similar house in the neighborhood for $1,000 per month.

As professor White explains, "Assuming they intend to stay in their home ten years, [the couple] would save approximately $340,000 by walking away, including a monthly savings of at least $1,700 on rent versus mortgage payments, even after factoring in the mortgage interest tax deduction."

It would take 60 years for the couple to recover their equity assuming that the Salinas, California market had hit bottom and the home began appreciating at the historically typical rate of 3.5%.

So what's our young family to do? Or the bigger question is what are the millions of young families going to do: pay or walk away? And if mortgagees walk away en masse, will they be responsible for destroying modern American society?

First American Core Logic estimated that nearly a third of all mortgages (32.3% exactly) were under water in June of 2009.... That's 15.2 million loans, and the negative equity position totaled $3.4 trillion. A Deutsche Bank report predicted that by 2011 nearly half of all mortgaged Americans, or 25 million homeowners, would be "under water."

> **Despite the millions of homeowners whose primary asset is now a debilitating liability, the number of foreclosures doesn't match the under-water estimates.**

In a number of former boom cities, the vast majority of homeowners are already under water. A number of towns, primarily in the central valley of California, have current percentage of underwater homeowners exceeding 80%. Eighty-one (81) percent of all homeowners in Las Vegas were estimated to be under water, 70% of those in the Miami Beach area and 68% of homeowners in Phoenix owe more than their homes are worth.

Despite the millions of homeowners whose primary asset is now a debilitating liability, the number of foreclosures doesn't match the under-water estimates. In April of 2010, 337,837 foreclosures were filed nationwide. A record 2.8 million homeowners were sent a foreclosure notice in 2009 and total foreclosures for 2010 were expected to top three million for the first time.

Speaking on CNBC's "Squawk Box" show in October 2010, Joseph Murin, the former president of the Government National Mortgage Association said there were 2.5 million homes in foreclosure and another three to four million borrowers "on the bubble" or seriously delinquent on their mortgage payments.

But, foreclosures take time. In some states it can be months, in other states years. At this writing, reportedly seven million homes have already been seized by lenders. But with over 300,000 new filings each month (and growing), the estimate of six million properties that have not yet been completed as foreclosures may be conservative.

But if it's close to being right, the number is a fraction of the 11 to 15 million homes estimated to be under water right now. It is a wonder that the foreclosure filings are not double or triple what are currently being filed.

> **Nothing makes a suburban American family sleep better than knowing the military is protecting them and the wise economists at the Federal Reserve are making all the right moves.**

Government has built a huge stake in the housing market since before the Great Depression, starting with Herbert Hoover's "Own Your Own Home" initiative. Government has standardized suburban living through its mortgage guarantee guidelines. Government has provided the secondary markets to make 30-year mortgages and the securitization of those loans possible.

Owner-occupied housing not only provides employment, but each homeowner has a stake in their community and their country. An ownership society is a compliant society. Those with an ownership stake recognize the need for the kind of security that big government can provide. Homeowners have something to protect and look to government to provide that protection. And a big mortgage that takes 30 years to retire keeps the family focused on what's important—paying for their American dream. There's no time to be concerned with the size of government, there are house payments to make.

No one wants to lose their home to recessions, depressions, or invading Russians or Muslims. Nothing makes a suburban American family sleep better at night than knowing that the military is fighting the bad guys on foreign soil to protect their happy home while their jobs are made secure by wise economists at the Federal Reserve who are making all the right interest rate moves. And the more local cops on the beat keeping an eye on the neighborhood, the better.

Murin claimed that housing should be 25 to 30 percent of GDP and that borrowers must pay their mortgages to maintain confidence in this vital sector of America's economy. On that same program, Ken Langone, co-founder of Home Depot said, "I can't believe we live in a society like this," fretting over the fact that individuals were gaming the system before losing their homes to foreclosure.

So, while those in government and big business are singing from the same choir book, as the housing bubble has deflated the strategic default issue has libertarians divided.

For some libertarian writers like Karen De Coster, the numbers speak for themselves, "Walk away, free yourself from unnecessary bondage, and let the giant banks sort out the mess that they helped to perpetuate and swell," the CPA wrote on LewRockwell.com.

But other libertarians argue that it is a person's moral duty to fulfill their obligations: a contract is a contract. To not repay a debt is the equivalent of stealing. The lender held up its end of the bargain by providing the money for the purchase or refinance of the home in this case. Now it's for the borrower to make the payments as the terms in the note dictate.

After all, promissory notes don't provide an out for the borrower if the property securing that note falls below the amount of principal remaining to be paid off. Conversely, if the prop-

A society built and financed by continuous government initiatives is not a free one or a just one. And certainly is not a libertarian nirvana.

erty value soars and the borrower makes out, the lender does not receive any of the upside; just the principal and interest due. The borrower and lender aren't partners.

Private contracts are the bedrock of a free society, it's argued. If people are just allowed to walk away from their obligations with no consequences, what kind of world would this be? America's social fabric would be shredded.

But a society built and financed by continuous government initiatives is not a free one or a just one. And certainly it's not a libertarian nirvana. "Despots and democratic majorities are drunk with power," Ludwig von Mises wrote in *Austrian Economics: An Anthology.* "They must reluctantly admit that they are subject to the laws of nature. But they reject the very notion of economic law ... economic history is a long record of government policies that failed because they were designed with a bold disregard for the laws of economics."

The laws of economics have leveled the government's 90-year housing agenda and individuals should not be demonized for obeying those laws.

Double Standard

According to work done by professor White at the University of Arizona's James E. Rogers College of Law, underwater homeowners aren't walking away because they wish "to avoid the shame or guilt associated with foreclosure," and "fear over the perceived consequences of foreclosure—consequences that are in actuality much less severe than most homeowners have been led to believe."

"[T]hese emotional constraints are actively cultivated by the government, the financial industry, and other social control agents, in order to induce individual homeowners to act in ways that are *against* their own self interest, but which are ... argued to be socially beneficial."

So while lenders only seek to maximize profits, borrowers are "encouraged to behave in accordance with social and moral norms requiring that individuals keep promises and honor financial obligations."

Mortgages and notes secured by deeds of trust, are contracts. The lender provides money today in exchange for a series of payments. The money today is used to buy a house (in this case). In exchange the borrower agrees to make 360 monthly payments of a certain amount of money to retire the principle and pay interest on the amount borrowed.

That's it. These notes don't have caveats that if the value of the collateral falls, the borrower can (and should) give the house back to the lender, although in non-recourse states like California that is implied. Non-recourse meaning that the lender cannot pursue the borrower's other assets if the value of the home doesn't satisfy the note. Even in states where mortgage contracts contain recourse provisions, the cost of litigation versus the limited prospects for recovery keeps many lenders from pursuing judgments.

The borrower enters into the deal in good faith, not knowing the future of property values, his or her income, or what surprises might spring forth over the course of 30 years. The lender does the same, knowing not what interest rates will do, how the currency the note is denominated in will fare, and again what property values will be, or how well the borrower's prospects will hold up.

However, at least one lender has no problem walking away from its loan obligation. Morgan Stanley announced at the end of 2009 that the bank planned to give back five San Francisco office buildings to its lender—just two years after buying them at the top of the market.

"This isn't a default or foreclosure situation," spokeswoman Alyson Barnes told Bloomberg News. "We are going to give them the properties to get out of the loan obligation."

Morgan Stanley bought the buildings, along with five others, in San Francisco's financial district as part of a $2.43 billion purchase from Blackstone Group in May 2007. The buildings were formerly owned by billionaire investor Sam Zell's Equity Office Properties and acquired by Blackstone in its $39 billion buyout of the real estate firm earlier that year, Bloomberg reports. One analyst estimates that the buildings are now worth half of what Morgan Stanley paid."

Morgan Stanley's EBIT in 2009 was $7.57 billion, in '08 it was $39.81 billion and in '07 it was $60.7 billion. You get the idea, walking away from the five office buildings was a strategic default. There is no Morgan or Stanley losing sleep over these buildings and the encumbrances being walked away from. The shareholders of Morgan Stanley likely cheered as the company mailed the keys to the lender.

The fact is the shareholders would consider it the fiduciary responsibility of Morgan Stanley management to walk away from its underwater property loans. In an essay entitled "Natural law and the fiduciary duties of business managers," by Joseph F. Johnston, published in the *Journal of Markets & Morality*, explains that the "**fiduciary** principle is a principle of natural law that has been incorporated into the Anglo-American legal tradition; and that this principle underlies the duties of good faith, loyalty, and care that apply to corporate directors and officers. The **fiduciary** duties of corporate managers run to shareholders and not to creditors, employees, and other 'stakeholders.' "(emphasis is Johnston's)

The best interest of Morgan Stanley's shareholders was clearly for the company to walk away. Their note was non-recourse. The lender has no legal right to pursue any other Morgan Stanley assets. The fiduciary duty of the company's supervisors is the prudent management of company assets on behalf of the shareholders. Not on behalf of the company's creditors or anyone else.

Large commercial property owners believe it only makes sense to walk away when their properties are upside-down to the loan balance. As Kris Hudson and A. D. Pruitt wrote

> **While big real estate companies are praised for making the good business decision to walk away, individual home-owners are vilified if they do the same.**

for the *Wall Street Journal* in August 2010, some of the titans of the commercial property business like Macerich Co., Simon Property Group Inc., and Vornado Realty Trust have defaulted on large property loans because of the fall in collateral values. "These companies all have piles of cash to make the payments. They are simply opting to default because they believe it makes good business sense," Hudson and Pruitt write.

Vornado may be one of the nation's largest owners of office buildings and shopping malls, but when the value of the Cannery at Del Monte Square project in San Francisco plummeted, the company defaulted on the $18 million loan on the project. Macerich gave the Valley View Center mall in Dallas to the lender rather than continuing to pay the $135 million mortgage.

Like homeowners who walk away, Robert Taubman, CEO of Taubman Centers, Inc., told the *WSJ*, "We don't do this lightly," when his company stopped making payments on its $135 million mortgage secured by the Pier Shops at Caesars in Atlantic City, N.J., after the property value fell to $52 million.

At the same time, former Treasury Secretary Henry M. Paulson Jr. declared that "any homeowner who can afford his mortgage payment but chooses to walk away from an underwater property is simply a speculator—and one who is not honoring his obligation."

John Courson, president and C.E.O. of the Mortgage Bankers Association, told the *Wall Street Journal* that homeowners who default on their mortgages should think about the "message" they will send to "their family and their kids and their friends."

"Please consider that those withdrawing money from their 401(k) to pay mortgage and tuition expenses may be the remaining righteous souls of this nation," a reader of Agora Financial's "5 Minute Forecast" wrote. "They signed a legally binding contract and are doing their best to uphold their end of the deal. They want their children to have a better future than they have. When those honorable and loving citizens are no longer praised for their morals and ethics and, instead, are labeled as stupid, what will be left?"

So while the Morgan Stanleys and Robert Taubmans of the world make the prudent business decision to walk away from a bad deal and doing so improves company cash flow, Secretary Paulson, Mr. Courson and other high-minded folks believe our would-be couple in Salinas— or anyone else who is under water on their mortgage—should buck up and keep paying—until they lose their job, exhaust all savings, or die: then it's OK if they bail.

Just Who is The Lender?

It seems to be a lousy bet on both sides: neither possesses a crystal ball that will remain clear for 30 years. In a free market, libertarian world would lenders make such a deal, or borrowers for that matter?

But the fact is that while the borrower is making a 30-year commitment, the mortgage originator likely isn't. The banks are holding these loans "for more like thirty seconds or thirty minutes," financial author Roger Lowenstein told Aaron Task on Yahoo! Finance. "The mortgages are immediately flipped to someone else. Why should the homeowner make anything but a cold, calculated business decision."

In the fourth quarter of 2010, Bank of America and other lenders stopped foreclosures and attorney generals in all 50 states opened investigations to determine if there was wide-spread foreclosure fraud. The Achilles heel of securitization, that had been such a boon to Wall Street and the mortgage originators in the housing boom, was revealed by the crash.

"In essence, fast-paced modern finance is colliding with the much slower machinery of the U.S. legal system," reported the *Wall Street Journal* on the front page on its October 16–17th edition. "While finance aims for efficiency and maximized profits, the courts demand due process. And that's becoming the growing issue as lenders come under attack for taking shortcuts to oust homeowners who haven't mailed in a mortgage check for months."

As homeowners defaulted en masse, their lawyers were quick to determine that the "robo-signers" which were approving hundreds of foreclosure documents each day couldn't possibly have been reviewing them, meaning the banks had not properly proved ownership of the loans.

More importantly, it was nearly impossible to determine whether lenders had the legal standing to foreclose in the case of mortgages bundled together into securitized debt pools.

Real estate law requires the physical transfer of loan documents and loan sale assumption agreements. In the heady days of the housing boom it is questionable that all the paperwork and loan documents were transferred properly during each step of the securitization

Securitization, with the slicing and dicing of mortgages into MBS products has made it impossible to know who owns the actual physical promissory notes.

process or in the case where loans were sold numerous times. And if the paperwork was not transferred properly, "the whole system comes to a halt," Georgetown law professor Adam Levitin told the *WSJ*.

Blogger Gonzalo Lira explained the foreclosure issues faced by the banking industry due to securitization in a lengthy post that was reprinted widely on the web with and without attribution.

The colorful Lira emphasized that only the holder of the actual paper and ink signed note has the standing to file foreclosure and evict homeowners. Not so many years ago this wasn't an issue because the savings and loan down the street made the loan and kept it on its books.

Securitization changed all of that as local mortgage originators sold the loans and the loans became part of mortgage-backed securities (MBS). The paperwork got sloppy with all of this selling and packaging.

Lira explained that the purpose for these MBS was to appeal to the risk appetites of a variety of investors; from those that wanted super-safe no-brainers to dicer paper sporting higher yields. To accomplish this, the loans were bundled into real estate mortgage investment conduits (REMICs) and carved into tranches to be marketed to investors.

Mortgages thought to be the safest were put into one tranche, riskier paper in another, adjustable rate loans in another, and so on. The combinations were only limited by the creative genius of Wall Street salesman and underwriters.

The tranches that would absorb the last losses would be pitched to the ratings agency to be called AAA and sold to investors demanding paper with that rating. First default tranches would be rated junk and the yields would reflect that.

Of course the problem presents itself very quickly. No one knew which loans would default first. The mortgages were all good going in, but when the housing market crashed and loans began to default en masse, the question was: "But who were the owners of the junior-tranche bond and the senior-tranche bonds?" asks Lira. "Two different people. Therefore, the mortgage note was not actually signed over to the bond holder. In fact, it couldn't be signed over. Because, again, since no one knew which mortgage would default first, it was impossible to assign a specific mortgage to a specific bond."

Fannie Mae and Freddie Mac created the Mortgage Electronic Registration System (MERS) to deal with this problem. The MERS system would direct defaulting mortgages to the proper tranche. MERS sliced and diced the digitized mortgage notes. But MERS didn't have possession of any of the actual notes And while the REMICs should have held the notes, but "the REMICs had to be 'bankruptcy remote,' writes Lira in order to get the precious ratings needed to peddle mortgage-backed securities to institutional investors."

It is between REMICs and MERS that the chain of title to the notes was severed. And a foreclosing lender must have proof by way of properly endorsed assignments of those notes in order to have the standing necessary to foreclose.

And a broken chain of title, in Lira's view, means the borrower doesn't know who the lender is and who he or she should pay. And if you don't know who you owe, you don't owe anyone.

Of course none of this made a difference until the housing bubble popped and the number of defaults skyrocketed. No one till now has been backtracking to see if the foreclosing banks have their paperwork in order. As Lira explains, this meltdown has caught a much smarter, savvier group of borrowers in its wake. They won't lose their homes without hiring a lawyer and putting up a fight.

The banks started foreclosing in a hurry by using foreclosure mill law firms and these firms spotted the broken chain of title, and in Lira's opinion (and others), "did actually, deliberately, and categorically fake and falsify documents, in order to expedite these foreclosures and evictions. Yves Smith at Naked Capitalism, who has been all over this story, put up a price list for this 'service' from a company called DocX... yes, a price list for forged documents. Talk about your one-stop shopping!"

Title companies started refusing to insure the titles of these foreclosures for fear that they would be stuck with millions in liability if the foreclosures were found to be not up to snuff. That's when all fifty Attorney Generals around the country began to take notice and call for investigations.

The banking lobbyists quickly got the Interstate Recognition of Notarizations Act passed by Congress which would have made the fraudulent documents good to go. However, recognizing the likely constitutional challenge of the bill and the political heat within days of the mid-term elections, President Obama pocket vetoed the bill.

The mortgage mess was coming back to bite the banks again. The fraudulent foreclosures would make all mortgage payers think twice about paying. "This is a major, major crisis," wrote Lira. "The Lehman bankruptcy could be a spring rain compared to this hurricane. And if this isn't handled right ... and handled right quick, in the next couple of weeks at the outside ... this crisis could also spell the end of the mortgage business altogether. Of banking altogether. Hell, of civil society. What do you think happens in a country when the citizens realize they don't need to pay their debts?"

Commenting on Lira's post, financial author and analyst John Mauldin wrote that the chain-of-title foreclosure mess should not be allowed to bring the system down. "Let's be very clear," Mauldin wrote on InvestorsInsight.com. "If we cannot securitize mortgages, there is no mortgage market. We cannot go back to where lenders warehoused the notes. It would take a decade to build that infrastructure. In the meantime, housing prices are devastated."

American sports marketing executive and social scientist turned consumer and investor advocate and activist, Nye La Valle analogized the foreclosure problem this way:

> This may sound crude, but it's the only analogy that's easy for people and judges to understand. A woman goes to a party or is promiscuous and sleeps with 6 men in a night or week. The following week she is pregnant.
>
> There is one man who is the best-looking, strongest, in best shape and richest of them all, so she wants him to be the daddy. Two other men, who find out she's pregnant, claim paternity. NOW, before the age of DNA and computers and all, it was simply someone's word and testimony against another.
>
> However, with the advent of DNA testing and sequencing genes, we can tell who the daddy is.
>
> So, a judge would understand the following:

> Judge, this has been a very promiscuous note. It's gotten around (transferred, pledged, sold, assigned) quite a bit and it never used protection (recording in public records, assignments, or proper endorsements). After being with at least a dozen different partners, our note is now pregnant (ripe for pay off/liquidation).
>
> The MOM (MERS, servicers) says Daddy #1 is the daddy, but the baby (original note) has blond hair and blue eyes judge, but the mom and claimed dad are both dark hair and dark eyes so we're suspicious.
>
> Two dark hair and brown eyes men come forward and state: Judge, we both slept with this woman during the time she claimed to be pregnant. Now, 3 different men have potential paternity.
>
> NOW, THE ONLY WAY you can determine who the father (holder in due course) is to take blood samples (accounting, servicing, custody, investor reports and data) from EACH MAN (servicer/transferee, etc.) to see whose DNA it was and all the others to determine the dad and who owes child support.
>
> Unless you do the DNA (forensic accounting analysis of all docs and records), it doesn't matter what the bank lawyers or servicers say really transpired here!

> Without seeing where that NOTE (not mortgage) came on and off anyone's books; how it was endorsed and when; who has possession and custody and who negotiated the note and PAID for it, you'll never be able to answer the age old question, "WHO'S YOUR DADDY?"

The *New York Times*'s Gretchen Morgenson reported in October 2010 that in Florida it was standard practice to destroy original notes when the loan file was converted to an electronic one, "to avoid confusion."

"But because most securitizations state that a complete loan file must contain the original note," Morgenson wrote, "some trust experts wonder whether an electronic image would satisfy that requirement."

Real estate attorney Michael Pines speculated on Dylan Ratigan's show on MSNBC, "that nobody in this country knows for sure who owns any real estate, residential or commercial" because of securitization.

Fannie Mae and Freddie Mac began putting mortgages back to big lenders like Bank of America because the loan files didn't meet representations and warranties.

Bank analyst Chris Whalen surfaced another problem to Larry Kudlow on Kudlow's CNBC show that aired October 18, 2010. Whalen's supposition is that the mortgages that J. P. Morgan owns from its purchase of Bear Stearns were sold multiple times to different buyers.

Whalen said that government policies made each bank in the United States a loan production office and that Bank of America would be forced to buy back $60 billion in mortgages from Fannie Mae and Freddie Mac for failing to meet representations and warranties. In other words, the paperwork was not in order.

In late October 2010, Compass Point Research & Trading estimated that mortgage investors would demand the nation's banks buy back $55 billion to $179 billion in mortgages, while FBR Capital Markets took the rosier view that only $24 billion to $51 billion would be demanded.

During the housing boom, Fannie and Freddie became two of the largest investors in privately issued mortgage-backed securities that were backed by mortgage loans that were called "subprime" because less than credit-worthy borrowers were the mortgagees or the originating lenders required little or no documentation for the borrowers to gain loan approval.

As the housing market was peaking and began declining in 2006 and 2007, Fannie and Freddie purchased $227 billion in subprime-backed bonds. The losses from those bonds would be the final nails in the coffins of Fannie Mae and Freddie Mac, entities that were formally taken over by the federal government in September 2008 and by late 2010 had cost the taxpayers $148 billion dollars to keep in business with the Associated Press reporting that the tab could eventually be $259 billion.

In the first half of 2010, Fannie and Freddie had put back $6 billion in mortgages to the originating banks. Bank of America pushed back against Freddie Mac in late 2010 threatening not to send any more better-quality 2010-originated mortgages if the Government Sponsored Entity (GSE) didn't back off of its demands for buybacks. Bloomberg reported October 21, 2010, that Bank of America would start sending its mortgages to Fannie Mae instead. The bank didn't put the threat in writing, but got the attention of Freddie Mac's board of directors because the GSE needed "a steady supply of healthy new loans to climb out of their financial hole."

FOUR

The Government Gets Behind Home Ownership

In an America that was arguably much freer and much more libertarian there was no such thing as a 30-year mortgage. In the late 1800's credit for home ownership was not readily available. "Much of the lending that did occur was done by land subdividers, builders, brokers, local investors, or friends and relatives of purchasers," Columbia University's Marc Weiss explains in "Marketing and Financing Home Ownership: Mortgage Lending and Public Policy in the United States, 1918–1989."

Some of these loans were done by land contract, which is arguably the worst possible loan structure for a borrower because title to the land is not transferred until all payments are made. "Mortgage loans generally were only one-third to one-half the purchase price of the house and were for very short terms of one to three years."

Essentially homes were seller financed. Those who bought houses had lots of equity going into the transaction. But homeownership was rare. Only 27.7% owned their homes in 1890. So, there were typically only two types of homeowners; the wealthy who paid cash and working folks who built their own homes. As Thomas J. Sugrue, history and sociology professor at the University of Pennsylvania points out, "even many of the richest rented—because they had better places to invest than in the volatile housing market."

But after WWI, the federal government launched an "Own Your Own Home" campaign with the objective being to "defeat radical protest and restore political stability by encouraging urban workers to become homeowners," Weiss writes.

In his book *American Individualism*, Herbert Hoover defined individualism stripped of the "the laissez faire of the 18th Century." but instead viewed American individualism as Abraham Lincoln's "ideal of equality of opportunity" and "fair division can only be obtained by certain restrictions on the strong and dominant."

Hoover attached home ownership with independence and initiative, believing that an American must own a home to truly be considered an American. Disturbed that the 1920 census reflected a decline in home ownership, "Hoover offered a vigorous, new approach to the housing problem through the application of federal, voluntary, and business cooperative activity," Janet Hutchinson writes in "Building for Babbitt: The State and the Suburban Home Ideal." At Hoover's direction the federal government threw its weight behind four organizations to promote home ownership: the commercial "Own Your Own Home Campaign" and Home Modernization Bureau, the nonprofit Better Homes in America Movement, and the professional Architect's Small House Service Bureau. This concentrated effort served to foster, as Hutchison points out, "an idealized vision of American home life rooted in the ownership of a suburban residence replete with modern amenities."

So while it may seem that Americans by their nature have genes that make them aspire to home ownership, this notion is nonsense. Home ownership was sold to Americans with "carefully calculated governmental policies that proselytized Americans about the virtues of suburban home ownership while opposing outright market intervention," explains Hutchison.

It was during this era that the rise of subdivision development began to form. The National Association of Real Estate Boards (NAREB) provided an organizational framework for builders and land subdividers to operate during the 1920s and 1930s, writes Marc Weis in his book *The Rise of the Community Builders: The American Real Estate Industry and Urban Land Planning*.

NAREB became a powerful national organization with a seat at the policymaking table beginning in 1917 with the U.S. entering World

War I. The organization assisted with the construction of housing for war workers and the mortgage financing for those houses. The organization received another shot in the arm when Herbert Hoover became secretary of the commerce in 1921 and worked "closely with the Commerce Department's newly created Division of Building and Housing, as well as with other federal agencies," Weis explains.

With the government promoting home ownership and the emergence of building and loan associations (the predecessors to today's S&Ls, which operated much like Credit Unions pooling savings and making loans to members), the percentage of Americans owning their homes increased to 39.7% in 1920. But these building and loan associations paid high rates to savers and so in turn the mortgage loans were at high rates.

During the roaring '20s residential mortgage debt tripled, but "much of this financing consisted of a crazy quilt of land contracts, second and third mortgages, high interest rates and loan fees, short terms, balloon payments, and other high risk practices," explains Weiss.

Herbert Hoover pushed for mass home-ownership on a large-scale with the aid of government coordination and regulation of development.

The presidential election of 1928 had Secretary of the Commerce Hoover vs. New York governor Alfred E. Smith. Governor Smith was an ardent progressive, believing in the obligation of government to intervene in economic and social affairs, and a belief in the ability of experts and in the efficiency of government intervention. He had set up co-ops and low-cost housing in New York City. But the 1920's had been a roaring economy and Hoover pledged to continue the good times. Hoover won in a nearly 20 point margin landslide that many historians chalk up to bias against Smith being Catholic and his ties to the corruption of the Tammany Hall political machine. But Gwendolyn Wright, in her book *Building the Dream: A Social History of Housing in America*, writes, "it was private builders and middle-class suburbanites who won the election for Hoover."

In the early 1930's, with Hoover in the White House, NAREB had a key role in the U.S. President's Conference on Home Building and Home Ownership in 1931 and lobbied intensely for establishing institutions that would be the beginning of government's direct involvement in mortgage finance: Federal Home Loan Banking System, the Federal Housing Administration and a number of other federal housing programs.

Hoover's Conference published the first of 11 volumes of reports by conference committees the following year. The committee pushed two agendas in the first volume. First was the idea that "mass homeownership depended on large-scale, well-planned private development," but that second, these private residential developments "could only succeed with the aid of large-scale public land development, coordination, and regulation," writes Weiss.

Weiss writes that Community builders were concerned about the government exercising too much control over subdivision development. By 1934, the NAREB struck what they believed to be a good balance between private development and government interference with the fulcrum of this balancing act being the FHA. At the same time, the NAREB, through its Realtors' Washington Committee lobbied against prefabricated factory-produced housing which would have undercut the influence of local realtors and subdividers and also threw its political weight "against federal funding for any other approach to housing, including new towns and multifamily public housing in the cities," Dolores Hayden writes in *Building Suburbia: Green Fields and Urban Growth 1820–2000*. "Allied with the NAREB were the U.S. Chamber of Commerce, the U.S. League of Savings and Loans, the National Retail Lumber Dealers Association, and the National Association of Manufacturers."

Since then the U.S. has been one of the few developed countries that publically supports its mortgage market, Achim Duebel explains, with income tax relief for mortgage interest paying homeowners, and "public guarantees and regulatory privileges that benefit the mortgage industry. The approach is unchanged since the New Deal era of the 1930s when it was designed to rescue a failing private mortgage industry and fight the Depression through construction-led growth."

As professor Sugrue notes, since the 1930's Americans, "are a nation of homeowners and home-speculators because of Uncle Sam." The NAREB's "major effort to enhance the old game of land speculation with a new game of federal subsidy gained momentum," writes Hayden.

The Federal Housing Administration (FHA) was created as part of the National Housing Act of 1934, with the intent being to regulate the rate of interest and the terms of mortgages that it insured, or in the words from the FHA's first annual report, "to bring the home financing system of the country out of a chaotic situation." These new lending practices increased the number of people who could afford a down payment on a house and monthly debt service payments on a mortgage, thereby also increasing the size of the market for single-family homes. "FHA's mutual mortgage insurance plan, by virtually eliminating the risk for lenders, acted as a powerful stimulus for reviving mortgage finance, sales of existing properties, and new construction," writes Weiss.

The FHA quickly became the vehicle of the reality business to "enforce strict land planning standards, curb speculative subdividing, and stabilize and protect long-term values for new residential developments," Weiss explains. "Through the powerful inducement of mortgage insurance, FHA's Land Planning Division was able to transform residential development practices as well as play a key role in shaping and popularizing local land-use regulations."

It's no wonder modern suburbia looks the same in every city. With FHA writing the rules, small builders or what Weiss calls the 1920's-style "curbstone" subdividers* and "jerry-builders" were put out of business, making way for the KB Homes and DR Hortons of today. Buyers couldn't get mortgage insurance unless the subdivisions complied with FHA guidelines, so as Weiss explains, this "new federal agency, run to a large extent both by and for bankers, builders, and brokers, exercised great political power in pressuring local planners and government officials to conform to its requirements."

---

*"Curbstoners" or "curbstone" subdividers referred to those who subdivided land hastily, sold the lots and walked away, leaving individual property owners to build their own homes or hire a builder to build their homes. The result was neighborhoods with no continuity or standard architecture.

And while builders feared planning from local city halls, they embraced intervention from Washington. After all, city hall couldn't guarantee mortgages which expanded demand for their product, plus their friends in the industry were running FHA.

The hammer that FHA used to standardize housing and finance was its *Underwriting Manual.* Loans and the properties securing those loans had to be done "by the book" so to speak. After all, loans on residential property made by lenders operating in the free market were only willing to lend 50 percent of cost with terms lasting three years. FHA was to insure mortgages for 20 years at 80 percent cost (soon to be increased to 90 percent of cost and 25 years, and ultimately 30-year fully amortizing terms and 97 percent loan to cost).

Private property was fine as long as those in government could dictate architecture, house placement, and maintenance. The FHA controlled much of the residential land planning in America for decades all in the name of protecting collateral values.

To take this leap of underwriting faith, FHA placed great reliance on its appraisal guidelines that were designed to expose loan requests on inflated property values or risky properties. "Consequently in order to obtain FHA insurance, lenders, borrowers, subdividers, and builders were required to submit to the collective judgment of the Underwriting Division, who together with the technical Division determined minimum required property and neighborhood standards," Weiss explains.

The FHA's "conditional commitment" provided builders with the assurance that qualified buyers could obtain FHA financing. This conditional commitment was verification that the builder's entire subdivision complied with FHA's underwriting standards. With this in hand, builders could quickly obtain bank financing for land development and construction.

Builders were quick to take advantage of the FHA program because as Weiss explains, "conditional commitments were based on the projected appraised value of the completed houses and lots, community builders who economized on construction costs through efficient large-scale operations could in some cases borrow more money from the bank or insurance company than it actually cost to acquire and develop the subdivision. The business advantages of this arrangement for large developers were quite intentional on FHA's part."

Because FHA controlled what homes could be financed, the agency held extraordinary power. FHA controlled what type of homes could be built, the size and shape of lots that the homes could be built on, how the entire subdivision could be developed and where builders could develop. Those at the FHA considered zoning restrictions and deed restrictions as critical to maintaining home values. Private property was fine as long as those in the government could dictate architecture, house placement, and maintenance. The agency controlled much of the residential land planning in America for decades all in the name of protecting collateral values. The FHA even "encouraged covenants to maintain racial exclusion."

The builders may have been privately owned but their activities were steered by the hand of government in a velvet glove. "Land-use restrictions, modern planning and improvements, transportation accessibility, and availability of utilities, schools, and public services were all important criteria for risk-rating in FHA's *Underwriting Manual.*"

But like all regulators, the FHA would claim not to dictate development practices. "The Administration does not propose to regulate subdividing throughout the country," the FHA's *Subdivision Development* 1935 handbook claimed, "nor to set up stereotype patterns of land development. But in their handbook's very next sentence, the FHA bares its teeth, "It does, however, insist upon the observance of rational principles of development in those areas in which insured mortgages are desired."

"Unlike direct government police power regulations, FHA always appeared to be noncoercive to the private sector," Weiss points out. "Despite the fact that FHA was a government agency, its operations were considered to be more in the nature of private marketplace activity. Property owners and real estate entrepreneurs viewed FHA rules and regulations as similar to deed restrictions—private contracts which were freely entered into by willing parties — rather than as similar to zoning laws, which were sometimes seen as infringing on constitutional liberties."

But the FHA brass was well aware of their power. James Moffett, who headed the agency in 1935 told his Housing Advisory Council, "Make it conditional that these mortgages must be insured under the Housing Act, and through that we could control over-building in sections, which would undermine values, or though political pull, building in isolated spots, where it is not a good investment. You could also control the population trend, the neighborhood standard, and material and everything else through the President."

As the Great Depression unfolded, homeowners went under along with small builders and developers. But big builders and developers had the staffs to complete the FHA paperwork and harness the power of government not only to survive but to thrive. And both political parties were fully behind housing and affordable housing finance.

After all, happy homeowners were happy voters, with FHA-approved homes in FHA-approved subdivisions and tied down by conforming FHA mortgages, supported by a professionalized FHA-approved appraisal process that valued the homes supporting those loans.

The FHA's chief underwriter Fredrick Babcock wrote in the 1936 *Underwriting Manual*, "The best type of residential district is one in which the values of the individual properties vary within comparatively narrow limits." Babcock went on, "Such a district is characterized by uniformity and is much more likely to enjoy relatively great stability and permanence of desirability, utility and value ..."

Americans were to enjoy the freedom of property ownership but it came with the strings of Hoover's individualism.

"Our development of individualism shows an increasing tendency to regard right of property not as an object in itself," wrote Hoover, "but in the light of a useful and necessary instrument in stimulation of initiative to the individual." For Hoover, "the sense of mutuality with the prosperity of the community are both vital developments."

Individualism without the individuality. All for one and one for all, suburban style by the government's handbook. Perfect for Sinclair Lewis's "George Babbitt," a realtor and member of the local planning board, "an individual who instinctively conforms to middle-class values."* It is clear that housing in the United States has been circumscribed by federal guidelines since the depression of the 1930's," writes Gwendolyn Wright. "The government has set standards for construction, for financing, for land-use planning, and, to a certain extent, for family and community life."

In Ms. Wright's view, the government's intervention into housing was the politics of "desperation and idealism." The attitude was antiurban and pro-suburbia. A house with a yard surrounded by a picket fence was the place to raise a family, not the city. Buying a house in the suburbs symbolized the settling of roots, as opposed to the cramped apartments in cities. Since the turn of the century, reformers had condemned urban middle-class apartment buildings as human beehives "which fostered sexual immorality, sloth and divorce," writes Janet Hutchinson. "These Progressive reformers invested the single-family dwelling with positive moral and physical influences."

The ideal American home in suburbia housed a working husband, housekeeping mother and a couple of kids. The government's "Own Your Own Homes" campaign had targeted women with a letter campaign to women's groups. Rental apartment living was denigrated in the government's literature as being overcrowded, relegating women to anonymity. As Hutchinson describes, "this solicitation emphasized the historical importance of maintaining the 'tradition' as a 'genuine Home maker, *in your own Home*,' a single-family residence that protected women from being 'stuck in a pigeonhole ... classified like so many pieces of mail.'"

> **"The nationalistic vision of Americans invested in home ownership contained the promise of a stable, hard-working citizenry grounded in private property that would defend its own land and democracy from invasion by foreign influences."   —Hutchinson**

---

*From the "Note" to Babbitt, Dover Thrift Editions, 2003, Dover Publications, Inc., New York.

Business benefited with jobs created to plan, develop, build and maintain these communities. And a whole new world of consumption was created to make life easier to keep the house and feed the family. "This new governmental involvement that championed the private dwelling for Americans intensified the significance of property as a primary factor for evaluating the citizen's allegiance to the state," Hutchinson explains. "The nationalistic vision of Americans invested in home ownership contained the promise of a stable, hard-working citizenry grounded in private property that would defend its own land and democracy from invasion by foreign influences."

Writing in 1981, Ms. Wright explained that a "timeless quality lay over the suburbs. Everyone assumed that things would continue as they were here, with larger cars and more roads, newer houses and better schools, forever and ever. Real events have hit hard on both of these scenarios."

No wonder, as Dolores Hayden writes, "A very powerful coalition had formed, one with close ties to the Republican Party, but also a lobby the Democrats would not be able to ignore. A new era of suburban development would soon emerge, dominated by large firms with federal backing."

Government's housing agenda was given another boost when FDR created the Federal National Mortgage Association (Fannie Mae) in 1938, which created the secondary market in mortgages. Fannie Mae was given the mandate to help make homeownership more available throughout the United States.

These programs boosted home ownership in a hurry. By 1950, 55% of all Americans owned their own homes. By 1970, home ownership was 63%. After WWII ended, the boys came home and the economy boomed, the housing boom took flight. From 1950 to 1970, 1.2 million homes were built, on average, each year. America's housing stock increased by 21 million units or by 50 percent, and the decade of the 1970's saw another 20 million units erected.

This building boom, as Robert Fishman explains in *Bourgeois Utopias: The Rise and Fall of Suburbia*, had its origins in Hoover's housing agenda of the 1920's along with the government housing apparatus erected the following decade. "Financially, organizationally, and technologically, the roots of the boom were in the 1930s, for it was then that the building industry streamlined itself," Fishman writes, "both the Federal Housing Administration mortgage and the mass produced tract house date from that era."

Fishman goes on to explain that the builder-developer (or Community Builder) was born in the 1930s and post-war these entities could borrow all they needed from savings and loans to build tracts of homes on a large scale. "William Levitt with his Levittowns was the most famous symbol of these industrial style planner-developer-builders, but the real impact came when medium and small builders were able to incorporate these innovations everywhere on the periphery.

"The buyer, in turn had easy access to the thirty-year self amortizing mortgages that the Federal Housing Administration had created in the 1930s and which private lenders soon matched."

Fishman compares the financing of the post-war housing boom in America to the financing of the French building system in 1860 where massive apartment buildings were financed through "Haussmann's 'mobilizing' of capital through the Crédit foncier. Housing didn't have to compete with business for credit in post-war America, a "federally insured 'loop' directed the savings of small investors into savings and loan institutions, where they were channeled directly into short term loans for builders or mortgages for buyers."

Another government loan guaranty program was born in 1944 after WWII. The U.S. Department of Veterans Administration (VA) loan program was to make it possible for military veterans "to compete in the market place for credit with persons who were not obliged to forego the pursuit of gainful occupations by reason of service in the Armed Forces of the nation. The VA programs are intended to benefit men and women because of their service to the country, and they are not designed to serve as instruments of attaining general economic or social objectives."

Initially the VA loan program parameters were modest, with the government guaranty only covering 50 percent of the loan up to $2,000 for a maximum term of 20 years with an interest rate not to exceed 4 percent. However, home prices surged after WWII and the terms were viewed as unpractical. The guarantee maximum was quickly doubled and the maximum term lengthened to 25 years. From 1944 to 1952, the VA backed 2.4 million home loans for veterans.

Residential construction roared ahead in the late 1940's and in 1950 changes were again made updating the VA program. The guarantee maximum was increased from 50 percent to 60 percent and the amount was nearly doubled again to $7,500, with loan maturities lengthened to 30 years.

As the years and wars passed, amendments were made to the legislation expanding eligibility for VA loans and increasing guarantee amounts. With the Veterans Home Loan Indemnity and Restructuring Act of 1989, the veteran would pay a loan fee of 1.25 percent but no down payment was required and the loan fee could be financed. By the mid-1990s the VA had guaranteed over 15 million home loans.

Ginnie Mae was established to purchase new loans that the FHA would be insuring as a result of the Fair Housing Act because these loans were considered riskier than the traditional FHA mortgages.

Veterans may now borrow up to 102.15% of the sales price or reasonable value of the home, whichever is less. In a refinance, veterans may borrow up to 90% of reasonable value, where allowed by state laws.

At this writing, the VA insures loans up to $417,000 with no down payments ($1,094,625 in some high cost areas) and the borrower's monthly payment may be 41 percent of gross income as opposed to conventional loan underwriting that would call for mortgage payments to be 28 percent of gross income.

After the VA loan program was established in 1944, the mortgage industry didn't change until 1965 when the FHA and Fannie Mae became part of a newly formed government agency, the Department of Housing and Urban Development (HUD). Three years later Fannie Mae was divided into Ginnie Mae and a privately-owned Fannie Mae.

One week after the assassination of civil rights leader Martin Luther King, Jr., Congress passed the federal *Fair Housing Act* (Title VIII of the

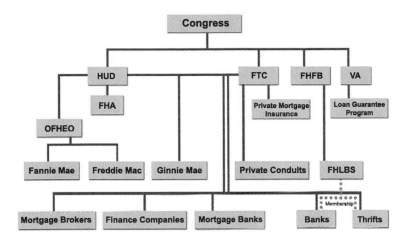

Civil Rights Act of 1968). The act's goal was "a unitary housing market in which a person's background (as opposed to financial resources) does not arbitrarily restrict access," writes Wikipedia.

Ginnie Mae was established to purchase the new loans that the FHA would be insuring as a result of the act. "These loans were considered more risky than the traditional FHA mortgages and so were channeled into a separate entity," Guy Stuart wrote in *Discriminating Risk: The U.S. Mortgage Lending Industry in the Twentieth Century.*

In 1970 Congress authorized Fannie Mae to buy conventional mortgages and chartered Freddie Mac to be another mortgage buying entity under the control of the Federal Home Loan Bank Board (FHLBB).

With the American public becoming addicted to credit in the 1970's and the Treasury looking for more tax money, the deductibility of consumer interest payments, including mortgage interest, became a target of the Congress.

Whether it would really make a difference for home values or not, President Reagan wasn't going to mess with the mortgage interest deduction, telling the National Association of Realtors in 1984, "I want you to know that we will preserve the part of the American dream which the home-mortgage-interest deduction symbolizes." Two years later, Congress ended the deductibility of interest on credit-card and other consumer loans in the tax-reform act of 1986, but left the mortgage deduction in place.

After the Savings & Loan crisis, the 1989 Congress passed the Financial Institutions Reform, Recovery and Enforcement Act (FIREA) which did away with the FHLBB with Freddie Mac's board becoming shareholder controlled.

Three years later, in 1992, Congress created the Office of Federal Housing Enterprise Oversight (OFHEO) to regulate Fannie and Freddie's safety and soundness, a job OFHEO either didn't do or wasn't allowed to do due to interference from the GSE's friends on Capitol Hill.

In 1989, the Department of Housing and Urban Development Reform Act "established over 50 legislative reforms to help ensure ethical, financial, and management integrity," according to *profile of HUD* published by the U.S. Department of Housing and Urban Development Office of Management and Planning in October 1982.

Jack Kemp launched his Home Ownership for People Everywhere (HOPE) in 1990. Kemp was Secretary of HUD at the time overseeing a massive increase in that agency's budget as it ladled out money for affordable homeowner initiatives.

According to *profile of HUD*, in 1991 more than 11.6 million households benefited directly from HUD mortgage insurance and other housing subsidies. "HUD policies affect the national economy through their influence on the mortgage and homebuilding industries," the report crows. "The entire population benefits as low-income segments of the rental community move to manage or purchase their properties.

HUD Secretary Kemp was part of The Empowerment Network that adopted the view of author Michael Sherraden, who explained in *Assets and the Poor*, that policies which he referred to as "stakeholding" were more effective in fighting poverty. Providing assets will lift more people out of poverty than sending them a monthly check was Sherraden's view. Kemp embraced the message, championing programs for public housing tenants to assume ownership of their units.

In their FY 1993 Budget entitled, *Expanding the Opportunities for Empowerment: New Choices for Residents*, the agency wrote, "Choice is really another dimension of freedom," with one of its primary changes "where housing assistance for the poor has been restricted to month-to-month rental properties, the Homeownership Voucher option will permit residents to realize the American dream by turning their vouchers and certificates into equity for ownership."

While Jack Kemp was trying to use government to drag the great unwashed into the homeownership tent, Fannie Mae and Freddie Mac began to loosen up their loan criteria to accomplish the same thing.

Edward Pinto, who served as an executive vice president and chief credit officer for Fannie Mae in the late 1980's explained in an article for the *Wall Street Journal* that aggressive mortgage underwriting was instigated by Fannie and Freddie after the Senate Committee on Banking was advised by Acorn and other community groups in 1991 that "Lenders will respond to the most conservative standards unless [Fannie Mae and Freddie Mac] are aggressive and convincing in their efforts to expand historically narrow underwriting."

Congress gave Fannie Mae and Freddie Mac a mandate to increase their purchases of mortgages going to low and moderate income borrowers by passing the Federal Housing Enterprise Financial Safety and Soundness Act of 1992.

HUD's National Homeownership Strategy championed looser loan standards and worked to reduce homebuyer downpayment requirements causing a chain reaction in the mortgage industry.

The very next year, regulators threw standard historical underwriting out the window. Forget about down payments, good credit, and adequate income to service a mortgage. "Substituted were liberalized lending standards that led to an unprecedented number of no down payment, minimal down payment and other weak loans, and a housing finance system ill-prepared to absorb the shock of declining prices," writes Pinto.

In 1994, HUD Secretary Henry Cisneros, working in the Clinton Administration, rolled out a National Homeownership Strategy that championed the looser loan standards and partnered with most of the private mortgage industry, announcing that "Lending institutions, secondary market investors, mortgage insurers, and other members of the partnership [including Countrywide] should work collaboratively to reduce homebuyer downpayment requirements."

A document entitled "The National Homeownership Strategy: Partners in the American Dream" was posted on HUD's website until being removed in 2007 and the following paragraph from that report illustrates the strategy:

> For many potential homebuyers, the lack of cash available to accumulate the required downpayment and closing costs is the major impediment to purchasing a home. Other households do not have sufficient available income to make the monthly payments on mortgages financed at market interest rates for standard loan terms. Financing strategies, fueled by the creativity and resources of the private and public sectors, should address both of these financial barriers to homeownership.

The looser lending standards had a chain reaction on the mortgage industry. Financial institutions had to compete with Fannie and Freddie that "only needed $900 in capital behind a $200,000 mortgage— many of which had no down payment," as Pinto points out. Private institutions did their best to lever up like the GSEs and they relaxed their underwriting to HUD's affordable housing policies.

By 1996, Fannie and Freddie were to make 42% of their mortgage financing available to borrowers with income below the median in their area. That target increased to 50% in 2000 and 52% in 2005.

Homeownership jumped from 64% in 1994 to 69% in 2004, the result of increased loans to low-income, high risk borrowers. So government programs have created the typical mortgage deal—an impossibly long term for which to forecast property values, interest rates, income levels and the like.

"There are two important phenomena to note here," writes Guy Stuart. "One is the prominent role the federal government has played in the [mortgage] industry since 1932. The second is the long-term tendency toward centralization of the industry, mostly as a product of the growth of Fannie Mae and Freddie Mac, though the consolidation of the banking industry through mergers and acquisitions in the 1990s has also contributed to this centralization."

At the time when homeownership was hitting its peak, the conventional wisdom was that housing prices never go down. Mortgage lenders evidently believed that because required down payments went to zero in some cases and negative amortizing loan structures required continued increases in home prices.

In 2002, then Federal Reserve Chairman Alan Greenspan poohpoohed the notion of a nationwide bubble in home prices.

> The ongoing strength in the housing market has raised concerns about the possible emergence of a bubble in home prices. However, the analogy often made to the building and bursting of a stock price bubble is imperfect. First, unlike in the stock market, sales in the real estate market incur substantial transactions costs and, when most homes are sold, the seller must physically move out. Doing so often entails significant financial and emotional costs and is an obvious impediment to stimulating a bubble through speculative trading in homes. Thus, while stock market turnover is more than 100 percent annually, the turnover of home ownership is less than 10 percent annually—scarcely tinder for speculative conflagration. Second, arbitrage opportunities are much more limited in housing markets than in securities markets. A home in Portland, Oregon is not a close substitute for a home in Portland, Maine, and the "national" housing market is better understood as a collection of small, local housing markets. Even if a bubble were to develop in a local market, it would not necessarily have implications for the nation as a whole.

The nation's deposit insurer and bank regulator, Federal Deposit Insurance Corporation (FDIC) published a report in 2004 that concluded,

> [I]t is unlikely that home prices are poised to plunge nationwide, even when mortgage rates rise. Housing markets by nature are local, and significant price declines historically have been observed only in markets experiencing serious economic distress. Furthermore, housing markets have characteristics not inherent in other assets that temper speculative tendencies and generally

mitigate against price collapse. Because most of the factors af-
fecting home prices are local in nature, it is highly unlikely that
home prices would decline simultaneously and uniformly in different cities as a result of some shift such as a rise in interest
rates.

Later that same year, in a report entitled "Are Home Prices The Next
'Bubble'?" senior economist Jonathan McCarthy and vice president
Richard W. Peach for the Federal Reserve Bank of New York wrote,
"Our observations also suggest that home prices are not likely to plunge
in response to deteriorating fundamentals to the extent envisioned by
some analysts. Real home prices have been less volatile than other asset
prices, such as equity prices."

When Federal Reserve Chairman Ben Bernanke was questioned
in 2005 about whether house prices might be getting ahead of the
fundamentals, he replied:

> Well, I guess I don't buy your premise. It's a pretty unlikely
> possibility. We've never had a decline in house prices on a na-
> tionwide basis. So what I think is more likely is that house prices
> will slow, maybe stabilize: might slow consumption spending a
> bit. I don't think it's going to drive the economy too far from
> its full employment path, though.

The same year Bernanke was testifying that housing prices wouldn't
go down, "economists estimated that roughly half of all economic activity was tied to housing," wrote Peter S. Goodman in *Past Due: The End
of Easy Money and the Renewal of the American Economy*, "either through
home-building, the purchase of housing-related goods like furniture
and appliances, or spending unleashed by people borrowing against the
increased value of their homes."

Echoing the words of Herbert Hoover, President George W. Bush,
said on June 17, 2004 "… if you own something, you have a vital stake
in the future of our country. The more ownership there is in America,
the more vitality there is in America, and the more people have a vital
stake in the future of this country."

In October of that year as the housing bubble expanded, Bush told
the nation, "We're creating … an ownership society in this country,

where more Americans than ever will be able to open up their door where they live and say, welcome to my house, welcome to my piece of property."

However, the ownership society came with a huge debt burden. Mortgage debt in the U.S. more than doubled form $6.3 trillion at the start of the decade to $14.4 trillion by the end of 2009 two years after the market crashed. Nationwide, the price of housing rose 86 percent. "The economy became governed by a new exercise in make-believe, the notion that housing prices could never fall," wrote Peter Goodman. "Still the responsibility for the housing bubble cannot be hung on any single person or institution. The bubble was the product of years of government policies that aimed to make it easier for more Americans to own homes."

Anthony Sanders at George Mason University wrote that GSEs not only pump-primed the housing market far beyond what the stated policy goals justified, but also caused more damage by actively helping to push up household leverage during the real estate boom. "Fannie Mae CEO James Johnson said in Q3 1998 that they were going to ramp up homeownership when it was 66.8%," Sanders notes. "Now, it is 66.9%. So, after trillions of dollars, a housing bubble, a banking sector crash, and a 90%+ market share for Fannie, Freddie and the FHA, we are back where we started. Not to mention about $6 trillion in wealth destruction. Can we politely ask that the Feds please stop screwing up the U.S. housing market?"

CHAPTER FIVE

Building Wealth by Never Paying Off Your Mortgage

It seems like a crazy idea now, but many financial advisors during the boom told anyone who would listen that they shouldn't pay off or even pay down their mortgage debt. Not only should everyone own a home, but everyone should have a mortgage and no one should ever pay it off. The conventional wisdom, built up from decades of government support for home ownership was that housing prices could never fall.

After all, those in power testified that it was so. Fed Chairs Greenspan and Bernanke, as well as regulators and economists with the FDIC and Federal Reserve Bank dismissed the notion of a price bubble in housing. Like all bubble markets, "the sidelines began to seem a place only for people who had an aversion to wealth," Goodman wrote.

So the days of mortgage burning parties were long gone. How stupid could a person be to pay off their mortgage? After all the home would build equity by itself, whether there was a mortgage on it or not and besides the money used to pay down the mortgage could be invested to earn much higher returns than the tax advantaged interest rate being paid on the mortgage.

The authors of *Untapped Riches: Never Pay Off Your Mortgage— and Other Surprising Secrets for Building Wealth*, Susan and Anthony Cutaia with Robert Slater claimed in their 2007 book that the fixed-rate mortgage was the worst mortgage in history.

The Cutaias claimed certain types of mortgages were wealth creators. Mortgages like Option ARMs, Cash Flow ARMS, and negative amortization loans were best because these loans were "smart debt" which freed up cash so borrowers could leverage their homes to create wealth. They also advocated interest-only loans.

To their credit, the husband and wife team cautioned readers not to fritter away their cash on boats and vacations. But, the adjustments on these adjustable rate mortgages are what set the housing crash in motion.

Never pay off your mortgage principal the authors wrote, telling the story of an 80 year old man with a debt free house and no cash. Thank goodness they were able to get him an adjustable rate $800,000 loan. Otherwise, "He might as well have been poor," they write.

The two financial/mortgage experts wrote that it's a shame to be debt free. They blame the banks for instilling the notion in our heads that paying off our mortgages is a

Financial planners and CPAs all over the country were advising people not to pay down or pay off their mortgage loans.

good thing, when in fact "being debt free doesn't help you build wealth. It just locks up your money in equity."

"KEEP YOUR MONEY OUT OF THE BANK'S HANDS," is the wealth-building strategy #3 from the husband and wife team. "NEVER PAY OFF YOUR MORTGAGE—NEVER!"

Scientist, financial analyst and mortgage underwriter Marian Snow claimed there was a crisis in her 2007 book, *Stop Sitting on Your Assets: How to safely leverage the equity trapped in your home and transform it into a constant flow of wealth and security.* Ms. Snow wrote that there is a high cost of forfeiting future equity earnings. Excessive down payments, amortizing loans, extra principal payments, bi-weekly mortgage payments and untapped equity from real estate appreciation were all sources of wealth laying fallow, wasting away.

Ms. Snow uses an example of a $100,000 down payment that instead should be "relocated into a conservative side account earning an 8% compounding return." In 30 years that hundred grand would grow to over a million bucks, she writes. Eight percent annually compounded over 30 years: only public employee pension plan managers make such an absurd assumption.

Snow the scientist then berates anyone who believes that a smaller mortgage amount means smaller interest payments and saving money. "Are you really saving anything? Aren't you forfeiting the opportunity to deduct more interest that year?"

Depression-era thinking has led people to the poor-house of a mortgage-free home and no other assets according to Snow. Ms. Snow's book contains all kinds of silly acronyms that she claims are trademarked for what she calls the *Home Equity Riches Optimizer* and the *Home Equity Retirement Optimizer*. Suffice it to say Ms. Snow's assumptions are aggressive and she dismisses the idea of a housing bubble despite her book being published in 2007.

It wasn't just real estate and mortgage hucksters like Mr. and Mrs. Cutaia and Marian Snow selling the mortgage debt snake oil. Financial planners and CPAs all over the country were advising people to not pay down or pay off their mortgage loans.

> "Planners must consider many factors when analyzing the 15-year versus 30-year mortgage option, but certain issues deserve mention. First, even if the mortgage is held to maturity, the argument that the 15-year option is optimal because fewer total dollars are spent to purchase the home is seriously flawed. The fact that a smaller total dollar expenditure is required for the 15-year loan is irrelevant to the maturity decision."

"Including a Decreased Loan Life in the Mortgage Decision"
Journal of Financial Planning, **December 2003.**

> "Advantages of the 30-year mortgage include lower monthly payments and accumulated wealth, in an investment account available to help alleviate hardships. Withdrawals from the investment account would be free of penalties for the non tax-deferred accounts, and free of penalties for the tax deferred.... The data showed that a borrower ... willing to invest with a risk level associated with the S & P 500 would benefit from a 30-year mortgage."

"Effect on Net Worth of 15- and 30-Year Mortgage Term."
Journal, Association for Financial Counseling and Planning Education, **2004.**

"The popular press, following conventional wisdom, frequently advises that eliminating mortgage debt is a desirable goal. We show that this advice is often wrong... mortgage debt is valuable to many individuals."

"Mortgage Debt: The Good News."
Journal of Financial Planning, September 2004.

"... U.S. households that are accelerating their mortgage payments instead of saving in tax-deferred accounts are making the wrong choice ... in the aggregate, these misallocated savings are costing U.S. households as much as $1.5 billion dollars per year."

**"The Tradeoff between Mortgage Prepayments and
Tax-Deferred Retirement Savings."**
Federal Reserve Bank of Chicago, August 2006.

Ric Edelman, who *Barron's* ranked in the top 100 financial advisors in the country from 2004–2010 and author of numerous books on personal finance, advised, "Never own your home outright. Instead, get a big 30-year mortgage, and never pay it off (assuming you can afford to make the payments on the mortgage)." Edelman wrote that our parents were all wrong to pay off a mortgage as quick as possible. Mr. Edelman's ten reasons to carry a big long mortgage are all over the internet.

Summarizing Edelman's ten reasons:

REASON #1 *Your mortgage doesn't affect your home's value.*

Edelman says the reason you're buying your home in the first place is because you think it will rise in value, otherwise you'd rent. Not having a mortgage is the equivalent of stuffing money in a mattress.

REASON #2 *You're going to build equity anyway.*

Paying down the mortgage is a weak way to build equity. The home will appreciate in value anyway according to Edelman.

REASON #3 *A mortgage is relatively cheap money.*

Debt is inevitable in today's society writes the financial expert, so load up on mortgage debt as opposed to credit card debt.

REASON #4 *Mortgage interest is tax-deductible.*

The after-tax interest rate that you pay on your mortgage is lower than other available credit.

REASON #5 *Mortgage interest is tax-favorable.*

Rather than pay down debt that is tax-deductable, invest that money in investments that are taxed as low as 15 percent.

REASON #6 *Mortgage payments generally get easier over time.*

Inflation will make your monthly payment shrink, relatively speaking.

REASON #7 *Mortgages let you sell without selling.*

Want to capture the increase in home values but not sell? Just borrow more against the home.

REASON #8 *Large mortgages can let you invest more money more quickly.*

The lower the down payment you make, the more you can invest in other investments.

REASON #9 *Long-term mortgages can help you create more wealth.*

Paying down your debt doesn't create wealth; put that money toward other investments.

REASON #10 *Mortgages can give you greater liquidity and greater flexibility.*

Don't tie up your liquidity in the house; keep it available for other things, like investments.

Edelman the hot-shot financial advisor claimed we should all stay in hock up to our necks and invest whatever money we might use to pay down the mortgage just in case home prices actually fell. While Edelman advised this, the stock market crashed, commodity markets crashed and interest rates on Treasuries and bank CDs went to virtually zero. During no time period could a person earn a risk-free rate of return higher than even the tax-advantaged rate of a 30-year mortgage.

Social Conscience, Fiduciary Duty and Libertarian Ethics

The average Joe and Jane are quick to sign on the dotted line with what they think is the American dream clearly in sight. Meanwhile mortgage originators are only too eager to facilitate the dream, knowing that a secondary market created by the federal government is waiting to buy the paper.

And why not? Eighty-one percent of people believe it is immoral to default if you can afford to pay. However, "9% are willing to walk away with a shortfall of $50K, 26% with a shortfall of $100K and 41% with a shortfall of 200K," according to Luigi Guiso, Paola Sapienza and Luigi Zingales in their paper "Moral and Social Constraints to Strategic Default on Mortgages" written for the University of Chicago Booth School of Business and Kellogg School of Management.

But even more interestingly, people who know someone who has strategically defaulted are 82% more likely to at least declare their willingness to strategically default. Plus an increase in foreclosed property in a particular zip code, Guiso, Sapienza and Zingales find, greatly increases the likelihood that homeowners will walk away.

"Overall, we find that the most important variables in predicting the likelihood of a strategic default are moral and social considerations," write the three professors. "Social considerations are directly affected by the frequency of foreclosures and the probability that somebody knows somebody else who strategically defaulted."

As the University of Arizona's Brent White explains, "the asymmetry of moral norms for borrowers and market norms for lenders gives lenders an unfair advantage in negotiations related to the enforcement of contractual rights and obligations, including the borrower's right to exercise the *put option*." A put option meaning the borrower gives the house to the lender.

Lenders are most often corporate entities run by managers with the fiduciary duty to exercise financial prudence on behalf of the company owners. These managers would most likely not view it to be in the best interest of the shareholders to negotiate with an underwater homeowner if the homeowner is current on his or her payments, because given societal pressure and norms, the prudent thing to do is for the lender to deny an attempted negotiation; historically, the likelihood is that the borrower will continue to pay. It is only when a borrower does not pay that the lender's attention is gained and negotiations begin. Thus, an underwater borrower must wreck his or her credit score, a reflection of their character and honesty, before a lender will negotiate.

So does the individual have a fiduciary duty to oneself? The short answer is—no. A fiduciary means "one who acts in the interest of another person," so by definition one can't be the fiduciary of oneself. But how could it possibly be that corporate entities have a duty of financial prudence while individuals have a moral duty to destroy their dignity and finances in the process of honoring a contract that lenders themselves would not honor if put in the same position?

Aristotle explained that man is a rational being. Man learns what works in the world, natural laws, to achieve his desired ends—survival and prosperity. As Murray Rothbard explained in *The Ethics of Liberty*, "the very fact that the knowledge needed for man's survival and progress is not innately given to him or determined by external events," shows that man has the free will to either employ reason or not and that an act set against his life and health would objectively be called immoral.

In the same book, Rothbard writes of "the perfectly proper thesis that *private* persons or institutions should keep their contracts and pay their debts." But the mortgage market is anything but private. *Grant's Interest Rate Observer*, in its May 14, 2010 edition points out that Fannie, Freddie and the FHA, "accounted for 97% of new mortgage lending in the 50 states. That is, they either purchased or guaranteed all but 3% of new homes secured by American dwelling places."

Now that lenders have learned the hard way that home prices can and do fall, they have abandoned the mortgage market. What private market there is for loans exceeding the government guaranteed maximum, the interest rates are considerably higher and the terms much more stringent.

Its hard to imagine that Rothbard would insist that private individuals be poorer and less prosperous by sacrificing to pay Fannie and Freddie, entities that are only in business because, as the White House quietly disclosed on Christmas Eve 2009, "it had," as *NYT* reports "in effect, given the companies a blank check by making their federal credit line unlimited; the ceiling had been $400 billion; by the following spring the government said it had spent $126 billion propping them up."

Rothbard goes on to make the point that, "Relations with the State, then, become purely prudential and pragmatic considerations

With government support, financial behemoths can hold out and play hardball with underwater homeowners, refusing to negotiate, while hoping the real estate market rebounds.

for the particular individuals involved, who must treat the State as an enemy with currently prevailing power."

Since Government Sponsored Entity (GSE) debt (Fannie and Freddie) is now considered government debt, as Rothbard says, the payment of this debt by taxpayers is coercion. So the funding these GSEs use to buy these mortgages in the first place is obtained through "coercion and aggression against private property." "Such coercion can never be licit from the libertarian point of view," Rothbard explains.

Rothbard advocated "going on to repudiate the entire [government] debt outright, and let the chips fall where they may." And in the same article Rothbard ridicules the Social Security Administration, because it "has government bonds in its portfolio, and collects interest and payment from the American taxpayer, allow[ing] it to masquerade as a legitimate insurance business." It is impossible to imagine Rothbard viewing Fannie Mae and Freddie Mac as legitimate mortgage businesses.

He went on to write that if the idea of debt repudiation is considered too harsh, at least put the federal government into bankruptcy. But, "we first have to rid ourselves of the fallacious mindset that conflates public and private, and that treats government debt as if it were a productive contract between two legitimate property owners."

Supposing that Fannie, Freddie and BoA had been left to fail, the mortgage paper the entities held would have gone on the open market to be purchased by investors. What price would the mortgages fetch? Certainly not 100 cents on the dollar. But with government support, these financial behemoths can hold out and play hardball with home-owners, refusing to negotiate, putting their heads in the sand hoping that the real estate markets will improve.

When BB&T Bank analyzed Colonial Bank's loan portfolio when negotiating with the FDIC over the failed bank in 2009, they believed the loans to be worth 63 cents on the dollar. When US Bancorp purchased the failed Downey and PFF Savings & Loans in 2008, it valued those loan portfolios at 68 cents on the dollar. Of course these acquiring banks would only complete the deals with lucrative loss-sharing arrangements in place.

Entities like Colony Capital and Lennar's Rialto have most recently paid (in 2010) the FDIC 40 to 44 cents on the dollar for equity stakes in distressed loan pools being sold by the deposit insurer and that's with the FDIC providing seven-year, interest free financing on half to two-thirds of the purchase.

The point is clear, whether the borrower is current or not, in the free market, a mortgage that is significantly under-collateralized would not sell for the full note amount. Buyers of these notes would pay an amount that would allow for a margin of safety from the collateral based upon current or the buyer's expectations for future housing prices. The buyer of these notes would have an incentive to restructure the obligations and have a performing mortgage. That's what would maximize the note buyer's return.

For example, Selene Residential Mortgage Opportunity Fund purchased the mortgage secured by the home of Anna and Charlie Reynolds in St. George, Utah for a deep discount, the *Wall Street Journal* reported in a front page story. The Reynolds were struggling with a $3,464 monthly payment and the value of their home had plummeted.

Selene, run by Wall Street legend Lewis Ranieri, "buys loans to make a profit on them, not as a public service, but company officials say it is often more profitable to keep the borrower in the home than to foreclose. If a delinquent loan can be turned into a 'performing' loan, with the borrower making regular payments, the value of that loan rises, and Selene can turn around and either refinance it or sell it at a profit."

Home values in St. George had plummeted in similar fashion to that of Las Vegas, only a two-hour drive away. Selene slashed the principle balance of the loan due from $421,731 to $243,182 and lowered the interest rate, reducing the Reynolds' monthly payment to $1,573.

"Around 90% of Selene's loan modifications involve reducing the principal," James R. Hagerty wrote in the WSJ, "compared to less than 2% of the modifications done by federally regulated banks in the first quarter."

And while many upside down borrowers can't even find a human to talk to about their loan, let alone sit down and re-negotiate terms that will benefit both parties, Selene immediately tries to contact the borrowers on the notes they have purchased, "sometimes sending a FedEx package with a gift card that can be activated only if the borrower calls a Selene debt-workout specialist."

One quickly realizes that what makes the Selene modifications work are principal reductions. Amherst Securities Group mortgage analyst Laurie Goodman wrote in late 2010 that 11 million borrowers could lose their homes to foreclosure if the mortgage principal was not reduced. "Ignoring the fact that the borrower can and will default when it is his/her most economical solution is an expensive case of denial," Goodman wrote.

A bailed-out lending institution such as Fannie Mae or Bank of America has no incentive to negotiate. And in fact the banks are doing nothing. The research of Whitney Tilson at T2 Partners LLC shows that of homeowners who haven't made a payment in a year, 23.6 percent haven't been foreclosed upon. Of homeowners six months behind, nearly 32 percent haven't received notice of any nasty filings by their lenders. Even 14 percent of mortgage non-payers of two years haven't been foreclosed on.

Bank of America's head of "credit loss mitigation" Jack Schakett during a conference call told the assembled analysts, "There is a huge incentive for customers to walk away because getting free rent and waiting out foreclosure can be very appealing to customers."

A typical foreclosure, he said, takes up to 14 months, and as a result, the number of strategic defaults is "more than we have ever experienced before."

"Loan modifications in Nevada particularly are a joke," Las Vegas housing analyst Larry Murphy told the *Las Vegas Review Journal*. "They are a waste of time, effort and expense for everybody—borrower and lender alike." RealtyTrac's Rick Sharga claims there would probably be fewer strategic defaults, if banks were more willing to work with homeowners in good faith.

An April 2009 change to FASB rules 157, 115 and 124 allowed banks to foreclose on a home without having to write down a loss until that home was sold. However, if a bank agrees to a short sale, it must take the loss immediately.

The federal government's Making Home Affordable Program (HAMP) was implemented in the wake of the crash to modify mortgages. The program was budgeted for $75 billion, but by the end of October 2010, the expected cost was $29 billion according to the Treasury's Chief of the Homeownership Preservation Office Phyllis Caldwell.

The Atlantic's Daniel Indiviglio made some assumptions and crunched some numbers to determine the cost per modification. Indiviglio found that the program had only a 41 percent success rate, but he assumed it would get better—50 percent.

He goes on to write, "But we're not done. Many of these will re-default. So far, HAMP's re-default rate is actually pretty good. Just 25% of loans at least 12 months old are 60 or more days delinquent. But as time wears on, this percentage will increase." A quarter of HAMP modifications re-default and Indiviglio thinks that's good?

The staff editor at TheAtlantic.com assumed a 40 percent re-default rate and ultimately just short of 530,000 successful modifications for $29 billion, or $54,757 per modification. This cost didn't reduce the principal of anyone's loan, but just paid for the bureaucracy to administer the program and push paper around.

"If you know much about mortgage modifications," Indiviglio writes, "then you know many are destined to fail."

The big banks are even reluctant to approve short-sales, despite this being the most cost efficient way to settle underwater mortgages. Michael Powell reported for the *New York Times* of a Phoenix woman attempting to do a short sale, where the short-sale price was only $6,000 less than her loan balance. The lender GMAC refused, instead choosing to foreclose on the home, despite the lender estimating that it will recoup $19,000 by going that route.

"Banks are historically reluctant to do short sales, fearing that somehow the homeowner is getting an advantage on them," Diane E. Thompson, of counsel to the National Consumer Law Center told the *NYT*. "There's this irrational belief that if you foreclose and hold on to the property for six months, somehow prices will rebound."

But Powell points his finger at the real reason banks don't want to approve short-sales: "an April 2009 regulatory change in an obscure federal accounting law. The change, in effect, allowed banks to foreclose on a home without having to write down a loss until that home was sold. By contrast, if a bank agrees to a short sale, it must mark the loss immediately."

Amendments to FASB rules 157, 115 and 124 allowed banks greater discretion in determining what price to carry certain types of securities on their balance sheets and recognition of other-than-temporary impairments.

"The new rules were sought by the American Bankers Association, and not surprisingly will allow banks to increase their reported profits and strengthen their balance sheets by allowing them to increase the reported values of their toxic assets," James Kwak, co-author of *13 Bankers: The Wall Street Takeover and the next Financial Meltdown*, wrote on his blog "The Baseline Scenario" just after FASB amended their rules.

The man who runs the world's biggest bond fund, Bill Gross, says the U.S. should go all the way to the "full nationalization" of mortgage finance. Pacific Investment Management Company (PIMCO) is among the biggest holders of U.S.-backed mortgage debt and Mr. Gross, PIMCO's head man, said at a housing conference in August of 2010, "To suggest that there's a large place for private financing in the future of housing finance is unrealistic. Government is part of our future. We need a government balance sheet. To suggest that the private market come back in is simply impractical. It won't work."

On the PIMCO website Gross amplified the comments he made on Capitol Hill.

> Later that morning, in front of cameras from my favorite television station, C-SPAN, I exercised (exorcised) my leadership role in proposing a solution for the resolution of Fannie Mae (FNMA) and Freddie Mac (FHLMC) and the evolution of housing finance in the United States. I proposed a solution that recognized the necessity, not the desirability, of using government involvement, which would take the form of rolling FNMA, FHLMC, and other housing agencies into one giant agency – call it GNMA or the Government National Mortgage Association for lack of a more perfect acronym – and guaranteeing a majority of existing and future originations. Taxpayers would be protected through tight regulation, adequate down payments, and an insurance fund bolstered by a 50–75 basis point fee attached to each and every mortgage.

Gross goes on to write:

> My argument for the necessity of government backing was substantially based on this commonsensical, psychological, indeed sociological observation that the great housing debacle of 2007–2010+ would have a profound influence on homebuyers and mortgage lenders for decades to come. What did we learn from the Great Depression, for instance: Americans, for at least a generation or more, became savers—dominated by the insecurity of 20%+ unemployment rates and importance of a return of their money as opposed to a return on their money. It should

be no different this time, even though the Great R. is a tempered version of the Great D. **Americans now know that housing prices don't always go up, and that they can in fact go down by 30–50% in a few short years. Because of this experience, private mortgage lenders will demand extraordinary down payments, impeccable credit histories, and significantly higher yields than what markets grew used to over the past several decades.** Could an unbiased observer truly believe that housing starts of two million or even one million per year could be generated under the wing of the private market? In front of Treasury Secretary Geithner and the assembled audience, I said that was impractical. Let me amend that to "ludicrous."

Policymakers not only have to consider the future "flows" of new mortgage originations, but the existing "stock" of mortgages already created. FNMA and FHLMC either own or have guaranteed $4.5 trillion of the $11 trillion mortgage market now on the books. As the Treasury contemplates the "transition" from Agency conservatorship to either public or private hands, how could private market advocates reasonably assume that pension, insurance, bank, and PIMCO-type monies would willingly add nearly $5 trillion of non-guaranteed, in many cases junk-rated mortgages to their portfolio? They would not. We are in a bind, folks. **Having grown accustomed to a housing market aided and abetted by Uncle Sam, the habit cannot be broken by going cold turkey into the camp of private lending. The cost would be enormous in terms of yields – 300–400 basis points higher than currently offered, crippling any hopes of a housing-led revival to the economy.** (emphasis is Gross's)

Gross told the *Financial Times* he won't buy mortgage bonds without a continued explicit backing by Uncle Sam. "Without a government guarantee, as a private investor, I'd require borrowers to put at least 30% down, and most first-time homebuyers can't afford that."

What Gross was saying, without saying it, was that the mortgage paper his firm was holding was worth a fraction of its face value but for the government guarantee. Allowed to go bankrupt, the mortgages that Fannie and Freddie hold would trade for pennies on the dollar in some cases. Gross also realizes that private lenders are not going to issue 30-year loans with little money down and may not make 30-year bets at all.

It is only with government guarantees and a taxpayer-supported secondary market that these loans become viable investments.

In *The Ethics of Liberty* Professor Rothbard constructs the example of the theater owner contracting with an actor for a performance on a certain date. The actor changes his mind and doesn't appear. Should the actor be forced to appear? Rothbard says no, that would be slavery. Should the actor be forced to reimburse the theater owner for advertising and other expenses? No, the actor should not "be forced to pay for their lack of foresight and poor entrepreneurship."

But of course if the actor has been paid and he doesn't perform, the actor should be forced to return the money. Rothbard points out, that problems like this are solved in a libertarian society by requiring the actor to put up a performance bond. "In short, if the theater owners wished to avoid the risk of nonappearance, they could refuse to sign the agreement unless the actor agreed to put up a performance bond in case of nonappearance."

In the case of mortgage defaults, the collateral to the property is the performance bond. If the borrower doesn't pay, the collateral is surrendered. A basic part of underwriting the risk of a mortgage loan is making "sure that the home is of sufficient value to cover the amount of the loan," Guy Stuart writes in *Discriminating Risk*. If that doesn't satisfy the debt, in most states lenders can choose to go after the borrower's other assets. Any deficiency or loss the lender suffers is from "their lack of foresight and poor entrepreneurship."

Some also contend that walking away from mortgages will lead to a fall in the value of other properties in a neighborhood and is immoral because the defaulter's action is harming the finances of their neighbors. As if we have a duty to our neighbors to do all we can to maintain and increase property values throughout the neighborhood. No one has that power. This is a similar argument that politicians use denouncing short sellers, that the short traders are aggravating price moves and driving stock prices or bond prices lower.

The denigrating of a neighbor's property value can be compared to besmirching their good name as in the case of slander or libel. As Rothbard explains in *For a New Liberty*, "What the law of libel and slander does, in short, is to argue a 'property right' of someone in his own reputation." But a person does not own his or her reputation and likewise, while he or she may own title to a home, a person does not own the reputation or reputed value of their home. The reputed value is "purely a function of the subjective feelings and attitudes held by other people," as Rothbard explains about reputations. The same goes for the collective feelings and attitudes in the property market. Just as "a person's reputation fluctuates all the time, in accordance with the attitudes and opinions of the rest of the population," so do the values placed on properties.

A similar argument is that strategic defaulters will increase the cost of borrowing for the rest of us. Banks will have to charge everyone higher interest rates on our mortgages in order to factor in the risk that many Americans will simply walk away from their mortgages if their house values crash.

> To sacrifice for the common good means trading a greater value for a lesser value. It requires impoverishment on the part of the individual to benefit those around him.

On the contrary, it's more likely that lenders will offer even lower interest rates to those with good credit scores and low loan-to-value and loan-to-cost loans because they recognize that home values can go down. As bubbles prop up inefficient producers, extraordinary increases in collateral values make all mortgage borrowers seem creditworthy. Why offer low rates and good terms just to the creditworthy when increasing collateral values make all loans good ones?

Crashes, depressions and recessions weed out the inefficient and the un-creditworthy. Loan pricing may actually be more rational going forward. The creditworthy will be recognized as such for performing during difficult circumstances and the loan pricing offered will reflect that. Higher interest rates will be paid by those who are viewed as less-than-creditworthy. Or the less-than-creditworthy will not get credit at all, forcing lenders to compete aggressively for fewer good-quality loans. This would force rates lower, not higher.

The idea that we as individuals are responsible for those around us conflicts with the libertarian view. As Linda and Morris Tannehill point out in their path-breaking anarcho-capitalist manifesto *The Market For Liberty*, "Since man's life is what makes all his values possible, morality means acting in his own self-interest, which is acting in a pro-life manner." The Tannehills point out that sacrificing for "the common good" makes man a sacrificial animal, a less than pro-life proposition.

To sacrifice for the common good means trading a greater value for a lesser value. It requires impoverishment on the part of the individual to benefit those around him. "Conflicts are produced when men ignore their self interest and accept the notion that sacrifice is beneficial; sacrifice is always anti-life," the Tannehills write.

A moral person acts in his or her self interest and in turn doesn't require others' sacrifice. The default moralist libertarian might claim that others *are* sacrificing if the strategic defaulter doesn't fulfill his or her obligation. But again the defaulter does not walk away without cost and lenders take an entrepreneurial risk when lending money. That is why lenders take houses as collateral for mortgage loans and don't lend the money unsecured.

But are modern lenders even taking entrepreneurial risk? The federal government has made sure that no matter how many bad loans they have, Fannie Mae, Freddie Mac, Bank of America and the other large, systemically-important financial institutions remain in business. As David Einhorn from Greenlight Capital explained in a speech given at a Grant's Interest Rate Observer conference in 2008:

> The owners, employees and creditors of these institutions are rewarded when they succeed, but it is all of us, the taxpayers, who are left on the hook if they fail. This is called private profits and socialized risk. Heads, I win. Tails you lose. It is a reverse-Robin Hood system.

Amplifying the point is bank analyst Chris Whalen who wrote on The Institutional Risk Analyst website,

> The policy of the Fed and Treasury with respect to the large banks is state socialism writ large, without even the pretense of a greater public good.

> Forget Treasury Secretary Tim Geithner lying about the relatively small losses at American International Group (AIG); the fraud and obfuscation now underway in Washington to protect the TBTF [To Big To Fail] banks and GSEs total into the trillions of dollars and rises to the level of treason. And the sad part is that all of the temporizing and excuses by the Fed and the White House will be for naught. The zombie banks and GSEs alike will muddle along until the operational cost of servicing bad loans engulfs them. Then they will be bailed out—again—or restructured.

So while borrowers are expected to make payments on hopelessly underwater assets until they go bankrupt, the lenders these borrowers are paying are not allowed to go bankrupt no matter the entrepreneurial mistakes that have been made. One has trouble seeing the morality in that.

When asked about the morality of strategic defaults many people will respond that it's okay to default if you can't make the payment, but if you can it's immoral. Similar to the "ability-to-pay" argument of those who support progressive taxation. Rothbard explained in *Power and Market* that the ability-to-pay principle of taxation cannot be justified with a logical argument. If the able are penalized, production and services are diminished, "and in proportion to the extent of that ability," Rothbard writes. "The result will be impoverishment, not only of the able, but of the rest of society, which benefits from their services."

How does one define ability to pay? Enough after-tax income with all adults working to service the debt and enough money left over to pay for groceries and other essentials? What if each adult can work two jobs making enough to service the mortgage? Or three jobs each?

Should homeowners have another family move in and have the families rotate to use the house, with the respective adults working opposite shifts (one set of adults working day shift, the other night shift). Many Hispanic families did this in a 24-hour town like Las Vegas during the housing boom in order to afford housing. Builders catered to these buyers in the lower-priced northeast part of the city by constructing relatively small homes (under 2,000 square feet) that were carved into seven bedrooms.

What should a person give up in order to make their payments? Food, education, transportation, funds to live on in old age?

During Weimar Germany's hyper-inflation, middle-class wives and daughters engaged in prostitution to keep a roof over their families' heads and food to eat. Is it a strategic default if the family females (or the males for that matter) do not sexually service clients for money in order to pay the mortgage? If not, one wonders why the default moralists draw the line there.

SEVEN

The Cost (and Benefits) of Walking Away

People that walk away from a mortgage aren't insisting that they should be allowed to stay in the homes that serve as the underlying collateral without making payment. That *would* be morally objectionable. Ironically, because of the legal chaos created by securitization and the bursting of the housing bubble, delinquent borrowers are able to stay in their homes for extended periods of time (sometimes years) without making payments.

Those who walk pay a considerable price. There are the costs of uprooting the family and possibly the stigma of stiffing a lender, but also in most states lenders to have the opportunity to sue borrowers for deficiency and thus attempt to seize other assets to satisfy the mortgage. However, the fact is the costs are high versus the potential gain from the sale of these assets, so many lenders don't choose to undertake that. But lenders have that option: to make loan defaulters' lives miserable for years as the lender chases assets to satisfy the debt. In some states a personal judgment can last as long as 20 years. And these judgments are transferable, so a big slow-moving lender may sell a judgment for 10 cents on the dollar, and suddenly the borrower must deal with a ruthless, aggressive and nimble pursuer looking to turn a profit on that cheap judgment.

There also may be tax implications to walking away. As of this writing, the Mortgage Debt Relief Act of 2007 allows taxpayers to exclude income from the discharge of debt on their principal residence through 2012. Debt reduced in connection with a foreclosure, qualifies for that relief. But if this provision isn't extended, those who walk away will have the IRS to contend with as well.

Plus, Fannie Mae, which now controls the mortgage market, is "locking out" any borrowers from getting a new mortgage loan for seven years if the GSE determines the borrower strategically defaulted.

Walking away from a mortgage will also have a detrimental effect on the defaulter's credit score. Not only will lower credit scores keep the defaulter from obtaining credit, or having to pay higher interest rates for credit (because defaulters are seen as higher risks, as they should be), but it potentially could keep someone from obtaining a job in the future.

If fewer people were able to over-lever themselves buying homes, that capital would be freed up for more productive uses—loans to businesses.

A Society for Human Resource Management survey reports 60% of their companies run credit checks on some or all potential hires. That was up from 35% in 2003, and a mere 13% in 1996, according to CNNMoney.com Even Transportation Security Administration (TSA) applicants for airport screener jobs are rejected if they have more than $5,000 in overdue debt!

A point that Murray Rothbard made frequently and that investor Doug Casey often makes today is that one of the benefits to American society if the U.S. government repudiated or defaulted on its debt would be that people would think twice about lending it more money. Politicians will waste money with impunity if the government can continually borrow.

The same can be said for individuals. Taking on too much debt to live in more house than a person needs (McMansions as they were called in the boom) is a waste of capital. Mortgage debt is unproductive debt.

Robert Prechter, owner of the Elliott Wave International writes in his book *Conquer the Crash* that the lending process for businesses "adds value to the economy," while consumer loans are counterproductive, adding costs but no value. The banking system, with its focus on consumer loans, has shifted capital from the productive part of the economy, "people who have demonstrated a superior ability to invest or produce (creditors) to those who have demonstrated primarily a superior ability to consume (debtors)."

Prechter made the point in the November 2009 edition of the *Elliott Wave Theorist* that banks have lent sparingly to businesses for the past 35 years.

Businesses report that since 1974, ease of borrowing was either *worse* or *the same* as it was the prior quarter, meaning that—at least according to business owners—loans have been increasingly hard to get the entire time.

The case Prechter makes is that banks have lent to consumers at the expense of businesses—and that it is only business loans that are "self-liquidating." Healthy businesses generate cash flow that can pay off debt, while consumer loans "have no basis for repayment except the borrower's prospects for employment and, ultimately, collateral sales.

"Banks have lent to consumers at the expense of businesses."

Lines of credit to businesses are provided with the understanding that the business borrowers will "revolve the debt," borrow to pay vendors and employees and then pay down the debt as their customers pay them for product. Thus, the debt is directly tied to the business firm's production. The funds tend to be borrowed only for short periods of time. Credit in this case aids a business in potentially earning entrepreneurial profits, which build capital, which ultimately fuels economic expansion.

Conversely, consumer debts are not self-liquidating, but instead stay on the banks' books for long periods of time, with payments being made only to service the interest and pay down very small portions of the loan principal balance. Also, as Hans Sennholz explained,

> [N]ew debt in the form of a second mortgage on a home may finance the purchase of a vacation home, new furniture or another automobile, or even a luxury cruise around the world. The debtor may call it "productive," but it surely does not create capital, i.e., build shops or factories or manufacture tools and dies that enhance the productivity of human labor.

If fewer people were able to over-lever themselves buying homes, that capital would be freed up for more productive uses—loans to businesses. Jörg Guido Hülsmann explains in *The Ethics of Money Production*, "The mere fact that such credit is offered at all incites some people to go into debt who would otherwise have chosen not to do so."

Hülsmann is writing in the context that fiat inflation makes borrowing irresistible and makes the point that as "soon as young people have a job and thus a halfway stable source of revenue, they take a mortgage to buy a house—whereas their great-grandfathers might still have first accumulated savings for some thirty years and then bought his house with cash."

Professor Hülsmann alludes to another benefit that would come to borrowers who walk away and have a harder time obtaining credit to the temptation to accumulate debt. Household debt has thrown "entire populations into financial dependency," Hülsmann explains. "The moral implications are clear. Towering debts are incompatible with financial self-reliance and thus they tend to weaken self-reliance also in all other spheres. The debt-ridden individual eventually adopts the habit of turning to others for help, rather than maturing into an economic and moral anchor of his family, and of his wider community. Wishful thinking and submissiveness replace soberness and independent judgment. And what about the many cases in which families can no longer shoulder the debt load? Then the result is either despair or, alternatively, scorn for all standards of financial sanity."

While it was not considered good news by most observers, Deutsche Bank's research indicated in August of 2010 that a third of Americans did not have good enough credit histories to qualify for a mortgage. According to the report, 35 percent of Americans had credit scores of 649 and below, including the 26 percent of Americans with scores below 600.*

According to Don Luth, Executive Loan Consultant at Hamilton Ladd Home Loans in Ridgefield, Connecticut, a 30-year veteran of the mortgage business, "for all intents and purposes, sub prime lending

---

*A person with credit score below 600 is considered a risky borrower, while those with credit scores of 700 and above are considered low risk borrowers.

has now been legislated out of business. So the sub prime financing options that were available to the sub 600 score consumer during prior recessionary periods are no longer available today."

"Mortgage holders do sign a promissory note, which is a promise to pay," writes Roger Lowenstein. "But the contract explicitly details the penalty for nonpayment—surrender of the property. The borrower isn't escaping the consequences; he is suffering them."

The simple fact is banks know that walking away from underwater mortgages is the logical thing to do. "American homeowners are now minimizing the human toll of losing homes and so forth," writes Whitney Tilson for T2 Partners LLC. "Purely as a group, on an economic basis, they're the only rational players in this bubble. They've pocketed $2 trillion in cash and now, when the value of the property falls below their debt, they're walking away."

EIGHT

Houses vs. Cars

It is argued that when one purchases a car on credit, that the buyer is underwater the minute he or she drives the car off the lot. This doesn't give people the right to walk away from their car loans. Why should a house be any different?

As a rule, car buyers don't structurally default on car loans. However, if the price of cars fell by half, and a person could buy the same car for half the price and cut their payments in half, there would be plenty of structural defaults on car loans.

Car loans are typically fully amortizing 3 to 7-year loans. The lenders know the collateral depreciates and they make the loan terms to reflect that. Up until the housing crash it was thought that homes only increased in value, and with the government's help the 30-year loan was born.

The financing rates for cars during the boom (and after) were lower than mortgage rates and the qualification process much easier: Most of the time it happens in a matter of minutes. No one is asked for their tax returns and pay stubs to qualify for an auto loan.

But there was no bubble in the price of cars despite the low financing rates. Cars are consumer goods. Homes, on the other hand, when considered with the land and infrastructure that is required are higher-order goods.

Austrian Business Cycle Theory dictates that people, as they earn money, spend some on consumption and keep some in cash balances, while the rest is saved or invested in capital or production. For most people, this means setting aside a portion of their income by buying stocks, bonds, or bank certificates of deposit or savings accounts.

People determine the amount they wish to put in savings by their time preferences, i.e., the measure of their preference for present, as opposed to future, consumption. The less they prefer consumption in the present, the lower their time preference. The collective time preferences for all savers determine the pure interest rate. Thus, the lower the time preference, the lower the pure rate of interest. This lower time-preference rate leads to greater proportions of investment to consumption, and therefore an extension of the production structure, serving to increase total capital.

Conversely, higher time preferences do the opposite, with high interest rates, truncation of the production structure, and an abatement of capital. The final array of various market interest rates is composed of the pure interest rate plus purchasing power components and the range of entrepreneurial risk factors. But the key component of this equation is the pure interest rate.

When government intervenes to lower interest rates, the effect is the same as if the collective time preferences of the public had fallen. The amount of money available for investment increases, and with this greater supply, interest rates fall. In turn, entrepreneurs respond to what they believe is an increase in savings, or a decrease in time preferences. These entrepreneurs then invest this capital in "higher orders" in the structure of production, which are further from the final consumer. Investment then shifts from consumer goods to capital goods industries. Prices and wages are bid up in these capital goods industries.

This shift to capital goods industries would be fine if people's time preferences had actually lessened. But this is not the case. As the newly created money quickly permeates from business borrowers to wages, rents, and interest, the recipients of these higher incomes will spend the money in the same proportions of consumption-investment as they did before. Thus, demand quickly turns from capital goods back to consumer goods.

Unfortunately, capital goods producers now have an increased amount of goods for sale and no corresponding increase in demand from their entrepreneurial customers. This wasteful malinvestment is then liquidated, typically termed a crash, bust or crisis, which is the market's way of purging itself, the first step back to health. The ensuing recession or depression is the market's adjustment period from the malinvestments back to the normal efficient service of customer demands.

The recovery phase, or recession, will weed out inefficient and unprofitable businesses that were possibly engendered by, or propped up by the money-induced boom. The recovery is also characterized by an increase in the "natural" or pure rate of interest. In other words, time preferences increase, which leads to a fall in the prices of higher-order goods in relation to those of consumer goods.

Homes are higher order goods, not consumer goods as one policy analyst contends who insisted that homes are instead a "durable consumer good."

While the factory to build cars is a higher-order good, the cars are assembled in a matter of hours.

It is the land that a house sits on plus the entitlements and infrastructure that are required before a house can be constructed that makes it a higher-order good, unlike a car. In a daily article for mises.org I explained:

> However, there is more to a house than the sticks, bricks, and gingerbread that people see and buy. The building of homes starts with the purchase of land. And buying land is not like driving over to Best Buy, whipping out your credit card, and buying a big-screen TV. First the developer and his staff look for land to build on because ultimately the builder believes he can sell houses on that land. Consultants are hired to produce soil studies and environmental reports, and to determine the availability of utilities and zoning feasibility. These reports take time to produce and cost money.
>
> If the land appears to be suitable for residential development, the developer will determine what can be paid for the land to make the project profitable, assuming his projections are accurate for the sales prices of his homes. After that, a price is

negotiated and escrow is opened. A hot land market will dictate short escrows of 90 to 180 days, whereas in a typical market, escrows of a year or more are not uncommon.

A key factor in how much is offered in price for the land is the interest rate to be paid on the loan used to purchase the parcel. Low interest rates allow the developer to pay higher prices. Low interest rates also allow for the developer to take on more political and development risk. The political risk is the uncertainty that the builder will obtain the zoning necessary to build the number and type of units contemplated when the land was being considered for purchase. In most large urban areas, zoning approvals—which ultimately lead to maps legally describing the building lots that the houses will be constructed on—take months in the best of times; now they often take years.

Horizontal development costs can change dramatically during this process, as city hall may impose improvements that hadn't been contemplated as well as cost increases caused by increased demand for dirt moving, utility trenching, and street paving. And since most of the costs of developing finished building lots is financed, low interest rates make more projects feasible than high interest rates, not only from a cost standpoint but also from a time standpoint. The interest for development and construction projects is financed—it is borrowed—just like the soft and hard costs associated with the development, thus the lower the interest rate, the longer the project has before it must be converted to a consumer good.

The comparison between cars and houses is not a valid one: it's comparing apples to not just oranges, but orange trees. Despite easy and cheap financing there was no boom in the price of cars. Nobody bought multiple cars with the idea they could flip them for a quick and easy profit. And although the buyer is underwater the minute he or she drives off the lot, the short amortization schedule in the loan terms aligns the value and loan balance quickly.

Interestingly, the modern terms of car loans are similar to the terms of home loans prior to the federal government's intervention in the home loan market.

Psychology of Regret

It's an old bankers' axiom, "your first loss is your best loss." Or put another way, don't follow good money after bad. The same applies to homeowners. As hard as it is emotionally to do, walking away from the down-payment you made going in when you purchased and the monthly payments made were your best loss. Feeding the loss by making payments each month is just spending good money after bad.

Based upon personal account from 350 underwater homeowners, The University of Arizona's Prof. Brent White contends that the decision to strategically default is driven by emotion and defaulters are not *homo economicus*. In his paper "Walking Away: The Emotional Drivers of Strategic Default," White writes that the elderly, the highly-educated and those with high credit scores are more likely to walk away. Most all attempt to negotiate a modification with their lender and are turned away at the door because they are current on their payments or if they are invited to pursue a modification, the "process turns out, however, to be immensely frustrating and ultimately unsuccessful for many homeowners."

Research has shown that investment decisions are driven by biases locked in the human brain and humans are especially loss-averse and tend to rationalize bad investment decisions. David Genesove and Christopher Mayer write in a chapter entitled "Loss-Aversion and Seller Behavior: Evidence from the Housing Market" from *Advances In Behavioral Economics*, "housing professionals are not surprised that many sellers are reluctant to realize a loss on their house."

These authors found that during the boom and bust in the Boston downtown real estate market of 1990–97, sellers subject to losses set higher asking prices of 25–35% of the difference between the expected selling price of a property and their original purchase price. "One especially successful broker even noted that she tried to avoid taking on clients who were facing 'too large' a potential loss on their property because such clients often had unrealistic target selling prices," write Genesove and Mayer.

And the cold, hard realities of the market are slow to change sellers' minds according to Genesove and Mayer. According to their data, lower prices and increased time on the market do not significantly influence loss-aversion.

Dražen Prelec and George Lowenstein believe that people do an accounting in their heads that affects their behavior. The linkages tying together specific acts of consumption with specific payments "generates pleasure or pain depending on whether the accounts are in the red or in the black." In an article entitled "The Red and the Black: Mental Accounting of Savings and Debt" which appeared as a chapter in *Exotic Preferences: Behavioral Economics and Human Motivation*, the authors' modeling predicts that most people are debt averse and show "that people generally like sequences of events that improve over time and dislike sequences that deteriorate."

Prelec and Lowenstein's work reflects a preference for prepayment, making the enjoyment of the purchased product unencumbered. They write, "one might want to avoid the unpleasant experience of paying for consumption that has already been enjoyed," and point out that a major economic loss diminishes subsequent utility from consumption. Just as utility from consumption is undermined by the disutility of making payments, the disutility of making payments is buffered by the *imputed benefit* derived from each payment.

The work of these behavioral economists helps shed light on why some homeowners who are underwater keep paying. They believe the benefits of staying and consuming (if you will) the house outweigh the amount of the payment. But when the hole becomes too deep the increasing numbers of borrowers begin to feel like they are paying for nothing. They don't feel the benefit of increasing equity, but only the pain of making the monthly payment.

Economist Richard Thaler has found that people are irrationally regret averse. In an experiment where respondents had the choice of being a person who wins $100 in one scenario or a person who wins $150, but was just short of winning $1,000 in another, most people said that they would rather win the $100 and not have to deal with the regret of just missing the $1,000 windfall.

"People tend to experience losses even more acutely when they feel responsible for the decision that led to the loss; this sense of responsibility leads to regret," explains Hersh Shefrin in *Beyond Greed and Fear: Understanding Behavioral Finance and the Psychology of Investing.*

Humans distort and misremember past events and decisions, hanging on to losing stocks, unprofitable investments, failing businesses, and unsuccessful relationships, rationalizing our past choices, while unfortunately "those rationalizations influence our present ones," Michael Shermer writes in *The Mind of the Market.*

> **Underwater homeowners aren't walking away because they feel a duty to satisfy their lenders. It's because they don't wish to feel regret.**

While driving the author to the airport in Las Vegas in late 2010, a cab driver told of buying a house in northwest Las Vegas for $180,000 and improving it with a pool and landscaping. At the height of the boom it was worth $360,000, but had fallen in value to only $140,000 according to the driver. He owed $250,000 and while he and his wife were paying on the note, they quit watering the landscaping and stopped having the exterminator spray for bugs. He and his wife were attempting to do a modification "and would see how that worked out." But as we arrived at McCarran International, he said with certainty, "the market will come back in three years and then we can sell it."

Individual lenders suffer from the same ownership biases that borrowers do. Bankers judge their loan portfolio quality to be higher than it really is, just as homeowners believe their particular homes are worth more than the other homes on their block.

The way Duke University rations its limited number of highly-prized basketball tickets serves as an on-going experiment testing this ownership bias. This rationing process, explained in detail by behavioral economist Dan Ariely in his book *Predictably Irrational*, involves multiple students, is time-consuming, random and complicated. A Duke student may have camped out and completed the entire ticket ritual but end up empty-handed and watching the game on TV.

After a lottery was completed, Ariely recounts trying to buy tickets from those students lucky enough to win the ticket lottery and in turn sell those tickets. When he approached a dejected student who hadn't won a ticket to the final four basketball tournament, $175 dollars is the most the student would offer.

Next Ariely approached a Duke student who had secured a final four seat and wondered how much money he wanted for it. At first the lucky ticketholder said that he wouldn't sell no matter the price. After some urging he said he'd take $3,000. When told that was way too high, he agreed to sell his ticket for $2,400.

Ariely and his research partner Ziv Carmon talked to a hundred students on the buy and sell sides to determine the market price. The potential buyers (all of whom participated in the Duke ticket lottery ritual) would only offer an average of $170 for a ticket while on average the sellers demanded on average $2,400 per ticket.

As Ariely explains, as owners we "focus on what we may lose, rather than what we may gain." The aversion to loss is a strong emotion, Ariely points out, who also explains "that we assume other people will see the transaction from the same perspective as we do."

It's a wonder markets ever clear. And in the case of the burst housing bubble, the process was slow and painful, as government kept lenders in business though capital injections, nationalization and accounting rule gimmickry. With their ownership biases running wild, lenders were reluctant to make rational deals with their borrowers and the government enabled this faulty decision-making through force.

Underwater homeowners aren't walking away because they feel a duty to satisfy their lenders. It's because they don't wish to feel the regret of buying at the top of the housing market using too much debt. And instead of doing the financially rational thing and walking away, some keep paying, rationalizing that they are duty-bound to pay the note until the bitter end, but secretly hoping their financial acumen will be resurrected by a rally in home prices. A prospect that in many cities is hopeless.

At the same time, lenders are viewing their mortgage collateral values through rose-colored glasses, with the government backstopping their biased decisions.

TEN

Conclusion

"Economic interventionism is a self-defeating policy," Ludwig von Mises wrote in *Bureaucracy*. "The individual measures that it implies do not achieve the results sought. They bring about a state of affairs, which—from the viewpoint of its advocates themselves—is much more undesirable than the previous state they intended to alter."

Professor White argues that the current negative equity problem is "market failure," but of course this isn't a market failure at all, but the result of decades of continuous government intervention to promote individual home ownership and the financing of those homes. These policies have led to government standardization of neighborhoods and virtually a complete government takeover of the financing of homes.

Government guarantees have become the entire secondary mortgage market and gave birth to the securitization of mortgages that provided the incentive for lenders to relax underwriting guidelines going into mortgage transactions and the disincentive for lenders to negotiate with borrowers as market conditions and circumstances changed.

No libertarian argues that one has a moral duty to pay their taxes. However, virtually all libertarians pay their taxes. The penalties for not paying taxes are too harsh. The cost of government harassment is considered high by most people, eventually the government will place a lien on your assets in order to be paid and ultimately prison awaits those who thumb their nose at Uncle Sam.

You may say to yourself, "taxes are different than mortgages," no matter that housing has been a government agenda for nearly a century and that a 30-year loan is an unrealistic government construct. A person enters into a mortgage voluntarily, while we are forced to pay taxes.

However, people pay property taxes because they choose to own property. People owe income tax to governments on the state, local and federal levels because they choose to earn income. Sales taxes are ladled on when we choose to purchase goods.

This is not the Ivory Tower. In the real world, we know the taxman waits around the corner of every voluntary decision we make. So the rational person, seeking to better his or her circumstances, does everything possible to pay as little in taxes as possible.

Contrary to being considered immoral, libertarians consider paying the least amount possible to the state in taxes to be heroic. Tax money paid to the state wastes capital and not only makes the individual poorer but all of society as well. Yet some of these same libertarians contend that a person has a moral obligation to honor a financial obligation that is now owed either directly or indirectly to the state.

And while it's possible that virtually all libertarians would quit paying taxes if the cost was that their credit would be ruined for a few years, that some jobs might not be open to them and that they would have to leave a home that they had grown attached to, those making the rational economic decision to hand Fannie Mae the keys to their underwater houses are demonized as acting immorally.

Strategic defaulters do not set out to defraud their lenders by taking the money and running. They made their payments and watched the value of their property sink. They approached their lenders to work out a compromise to no avail. In financial self-defense they are forced to walk away. Libertarians don't believe in the initiation of physical violence, but they do support the idea of defending one's person and property from aggression. By the same token, these libertarians should support the idea of defending one's financial health and property.

These default moralizers expect everyone to live up to the moral standards of their utopian *laissez-faire* world, while on the other side of the transaction are government constructs that are maintained by force, violence and arbitrary changes in accounting rules. Ironically, the utopian libertarians end up preaching the same message that the big government bail-out apologists do—you must honor your obligations no matter what.

For individuals to make uneconomic decisions that are profoundly detrimental to their individual finances and well-being in order to make government bigger and more intrusive is directly contrary to the notion of freedom on every level.

There will be no salvation for those who sacrifice and put their financial futures at risk to remain current on an underwater mortgage. Whether you can pay or not, if it makes sense to walk away, that's what a person should do.

No obituary will ever read, "He was a good and ethical man. He died broke, his family suffered, but he never missed a payment to Fannie Mae."

To walk away is not a breach of freedom ethics. It might be the beginning of a rediscovery of those ethics, and a recapturing of the pioneering spirit of the old days, but with a digital twist.

We live in times when physical ownership is becoming ever less valuable as compared with the life we can create for ourselves in the world of digits that know no plots of lands and national borders. Just as capital itself became internationalized several decades ago, with great gains for freedom and prosperity, we might all follow that trend today, walking away from the mess that the state has made and creating a new life for ourselves that defies the impulse to control.

Index

About the Author

Douglas E. French is president of the Ludwig von Mises Institute. He received his master's degree under the direction of Murray N. Rothbard at the University of Nevada, Las Vegas, after many years in the business of banking. He is the author of *Early Speculative Bubbles* (Mises Institute, 2009), the first major empirical study of the relationship between early bubbles and the money supply.

Contact: french@mises.org